ALASKA
and the Airplane

A Century of Flight

BRAUN

Imprint

The Deutsche Nationalbibliothek lists this publication in the Deutsche
Nationalbibliografie; detailed bibliographic data are available in the Internet
at http://dnb.dnb.de.

ISBN 978-3-03768-141-1

1st edition 2013

Editorial staff: Katja Kolossowa, Manuela Roth
Graphic concept and layout: Michaela Prinz

Julie Decker | Jeremy Kinney

ALASKA
and the Airplane
A Century of Flight

Photographs by Eric F. Long

BRAUN

ACKNOWLEDGMENTS

This book is a project of the Anchorage Museum, in collaboration with the Smithsonian National Air and Space Museum. This book and exhibition would not have been possible without the gracious help of many individuals and institutions. *Alaska and the Airplane*, and the coordinating exhibition *Arctic Flight*, was a three-year project involving many institutions across a long-distance. We'd like to thank many people and institutions for their support and contributions:

In Alaska: Lowell Thomas, Jr.; Richard Benner; Pete Haggland; Katherine Ringsmuth; Lars Gleitsman; John Reffert; Shari Hart; Norm Lagasse; Gina Hollomon; Angie Demma; Chuck Miller; Paul and Donna Claus; Susan Morgan; staff at the Alaska Aviation Museum and Alaskan Heritage Museum in Anchorage; the Pioneer Air Museum and the Pioneer History Museum in Fairbanks; and the Carrie M. McClain Memorial Museum in Nome; and the staff at the Anchorage Museum, including James Pepper Henry; Jenya Anichenko; Nate Chambers; Julie Farnham; Monica Garcia; Ann Hale; Ted Gardeline;

Ryan Kenny; Carolyn Kozak; Darian LaTocha; Dave Nicholls; Don Mohr, Jane Rabadi, Sara Piasecki; Rex Schloeman; Monica Shah; and Christine Smith.

In Washington, D.C.: the staff of the Smithsonian National Air and Space Museum, including: Aeronautics Division Chairman Bob van der Linden; Curators Roger Connor; Chris Moore; Dorothy Cochrane; Tom Crouch; Dom Pisano; and Alex Spencer; Administrative: Collette Williams; Archives: Marilyn Graskowiak; Melissa Keiser; Jessamyn Lloyd, Mark Avino, Jelena Fay-Lukic; Collections: Douglas Erickson; Ken Isbell; Craig Brunetti; Katherine Watson; Carl Bobrow; Lisa Young; Ellen Folkema; and, Publications: Trish Graboske. And Valdi Stefanson for his consultation.

Julie Decker, Curator, Anchorage Museum
Jeremy R. Kinney, Curator,
Smithsonian National Air and Space Museum

FOREWORD

Alaska, over twice the size of Texas, is the largest state in the United States in landmass, encompassing nearly 600,000 square miles. It is a land so vast that approximately 83 percent of Alaskan communities are isolated from road service. Many of these communities rely upon small aircraft as a lifeline for supplies, mail, and emergency services.

The forty-ninth state has six times as many pilots and sixteen times as many aircraft per capita in comparison to the contiguous United States. A unique "bush pilot" culture has evolved in Alaska as a result of the heavy reliance on rural aviation as the only practical means of transportation and connection to and from the outside world.

This project reflects upon the remarkable history and evolution of aviation in Alaska over the past 100 years, beginning with the first powered flight in 1913. It honors bush pilot legends such as Carl Ben Eielson, Linious McGee, Russel Hyde Merrill, Noel Wien, and many others. The exhibition includes objects that are unique to flying in Alaska, and mementos and ephemera that highlight historic tales of aviation triumph, tragedy and survival.

Alaska and the Airplane is a tribute to the pioneer spirit of Alaska's bush pilots and the way the airplane shaped and continues to shape daily life in Alaska. We wish to thank all those who have contributed their time, energy, and resources to the *Arctic Flight* exhibition and this accompanying catalogue.

James Pepper Henry, CEO, Anchorage Museum

AVIATORS CAPT AND MRS. CAPT. JAS. V. MARTIN WITH THEIR AEROPLANE - THE FIRST IN ALASKA - UNDER THE MIDNIGHT SUN, FAIRBANKS, ALASKA, 1913
CLEMONS PHOTO.

Aviators Capt. James V. Martin and Lilly Martin with their airplane in Fairbanks in 1913 – recorded as the first powered flight in Alaska. Their airplane was shipped to Alaska from Seattle by steamboat across the ocean and up rivers. They introduced the spectacle of flight to merchants and residents of Fairbanks, but it was another decade before the airplane started to become part of the fabric of everyday life in the Territory.

INTRODUCTION

In July 1913, a group of local merchants was awaiting delivery of a large crate that had been shipped from Seattle to Fairbanks, the second-largest city in Alaska, then best known for marking the midpoint in all directions of the Territory. The crate had traveled from Seattle to Skagway by ocean steamer, then from Skagway to Whitehorse via steamboat, and finally from Whitehorse to Fairbanks aboard another steamboat navigating Alaska's Chena River. The sender of the package was a couple: James V. and Lilly Martin.

James Vernon Martin (1885–1956) was a Harvard-educated aviator and inventor who had served with the Merchant Marine and who in 1910 had organized the first international air meet in the United States. His wife Lilly was England's first woman aviator. James and Lilly were on the aviation demonstration circuit and their well-traveled crate contained an airplane.

The merchants hoped that the Martins and their airplane would bring a new vitality to Fairbanks and dramatize the city's potential as a hub of development and commerce. They intended to offer central Alaska something it had never seen before: the spectacle of flight.

The Martins, hired as aerial performers, assembled James's design, the Martin Tractor Aeroplane, from the parts in the crate once it was unloaded after the long voyage. On the evening of July 3, the Martins took off from Exposition Park, a Fairbanks ballpark (later named Weeks Field after Secretary of War John Weeks), and flew their biplane over spectators at an altitude of 200 feet and at speeds of up to 45 miles per hour, eventually making five flights in three days as well as lecturing on aeronautics at the Fairbanks Theater. During their time in Fairbanks the Martins tried unsuccessfully to sell their airplane. When no buyers came forward, they crated it up again and shipped it back to their home in San Francisco. People still were not convinced that flight was anything but a spectacle, in Fairbanks and elsewhere. The Martins' venture came slightly less than ten years after two Ohio bicycle makers, Wilbur and Orville Wright, made the first successful powered aircraft flights at Kill Devil Hill near Kitty Hawk on the Outer Banks of North Carolina on December 17, 1903. Although their longest flight lasted only fifty-nine seconds, improved aircraft and engines soon followed.

More than 3,500 miles away from those lonely Atlantic barrier islands, Alaska was a land of mountainous topography separated from the United States mainland by Canada. The state spans 1,420 miles from north to south and 2,500 miles from east to west. It has the most northern location (Point Barrow) and the most western point (Cape Wrangell) in the United States. Isolation and remoteness define Alaska, its wilderness often inaccessible except by air. The introduction of the airplane to Alaska was akin to the introduction of magic. Suddenly vast tracts of rugged terrain were no longer a barrier to traversing the state. While the Fairbanks aeronautical demonstration was not a financial success, it demonstrated that the airplane could address problems of access to the remote interior of Alaska. A natural air theater, its cities divided by virtually insurmountable terrain, Alaska relied on the airplane as its means of transportation, its supply line, and its source of emergency aid long before the rest of America took aviation seriously.

The year 1913 did not mark the start of aviation in Alaska.[1] The Martins journeyed back to Seattle as soon as they could with their unsellable airplane. With them went the fact that being the first to fly in the state was not all that important to the overall experience of flight in Alaska.

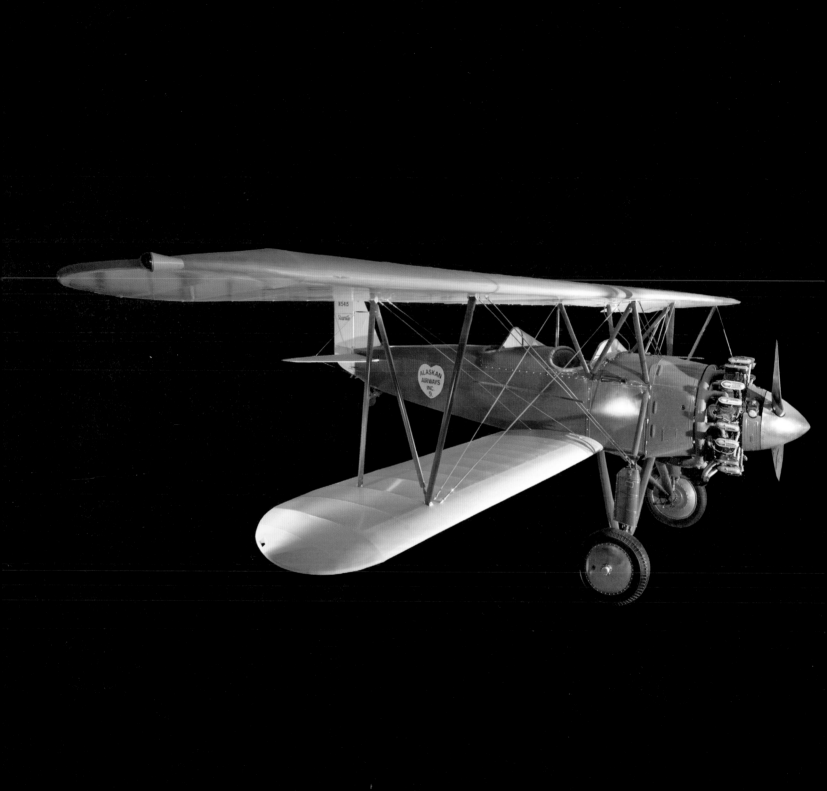

After the brief, but spectacular, introduction of the airplane in Fairbanks, no flying took place in the territory of Alaska until it became a byway of flight for the world aviation community in the 1920s. The inaccessibility of the territory was exotic to outsiders as they passed through on their way to fulfilling their dreams of a connected world. The airplane electrified Western society. It was a dramatic new technology that took humankind into the air and gave it the ability to conquer the sky, and with it, time, and space. In the United States especially, zealous enthusiasm for the airplane, called "airmindedness," led many to believe that the airplane would usher in a new aerial utopian age.[2] Identifying with their pioneer past, pilots, designers, engineers, entrepreneurs, workers, and everyday people saw the sky as a frontier to be settled with airplanes just as the American West had been with the Conestoga wagon and the railroad.[3]

While the world watched outsiders use Alaska as a global byway in the 1920s, airminded insiders adopted the airplane. These pilots and airplanes were not just passing through. Sourdoughs and cheechakos alike, expressing their own Alaskan brand of airmindedness, fought to conquer the air over what became widely known as America's last frontier. These daring individuals, who considered themselves to be "cowboys of the sky," but who quickly became

better known as bush pilots, were central to making the airplane part of everyday life in Alaska.[4] They connected the remote villages of Alaska by carrying mail, freight, and people and brought adventurers to the mountains, glaciers, forests, lakes, and other natural wonders. As the bush pilots opened up the interior of Alaska, airlines connected the territory to the rest of the world and resource developers arrived to reap the harvest of natural resources.

World events made the Territory a strategic bastion during World War II and the Cold War. American forces fought a bitter, forgotten, and largely aerial campaign to retake part of the Aleutians from the Japanese as the vital air route to Siberia delivered much-needed aircraft to communist ally, the Soviet Union. An increased American military presence led to the Territory (and then state after 1959) becoming a frontline in the Cold War. The use of military aviation in warfare, called airpower, is also a part of aviation in Alaska. Whether pilots were flying for commercial airlines, military units, or for themselves, they faced a constant in Alaska aviation that was not present on that sun-drenched and flat ballpark in Fairbanks in 1913. After 100 years, unpredictable weather, rough terrain, and long-distances have shaped the people and technology of flight in Alaska, while the danger of flying in Alaska has not been conquered.

Stearman C2B Biplane
Built in Wichita, Kansas, this Stearman C2B came to Alaska in July 1928. Its rugged construction, which included a tubular steel fuselage, ensured it could reliably be flown on wheels, skis, and floats. A number of well-known bush pilots, including Noel Wien, Merle "Mudhole" Smith, and Joe Crosson, flew it during the late 1920s and 1930s. Jerry Jones landed the C2B on Muldrow Glacier several times at Mt. McKinley in May 1932 in support of mountain-climbing operations.

BYWAYS

BYWAYS

In the early evening of August 23, 1920, a group of four airplanes appeared in the sky over Norton Sound near Nome, a bustling gold mining town on the western coast of the Alaska Territory. They successfully avoided a snow squall and swooped in over Nome. Over the rooftops, they dropped packages of mail for the town's residents, which were the first to be delivered by air in the Territory. Within minutes the four de Havilland DH-4B's of the U.S. Army Air Service's Alaskan Air Expedition, led by Captain St. Clair Streett, had landed in perfect formation on the parade ground at the nearby army post, Fort Davis. Prospectors, miners, and Natives from Nome and nearby villages came to see the sight. For many, it was the first time they had ever seen an airplane. Just sixteen days before, the Expedition was at Mineola on Long Island, New York. Their 4,300-mile journey across the United States and Canada to Nome was one of the most daring and dangerous aerial journeys ever attempted.[5]

During the 1920s and 1930s, the United States and Europe celebrated the airplane and aviation in general as an extraordinary achievement. Spectacular flights of distance, endurance, planning, skill, and speed by both military and civilian aviators facilitated this overwhelming public fascination with flight. In the United States, there was the airminded belief that the airplane would serve as a global technology, joining together all humankind. These dreams of a connected aerial world, whether it was a nation wishing a better link to its territory, explorers wanting to conquer the wilderness, or airlines creating an international travel network, ensured that Alaska would serve as an important aerial byway for the world.

The American military first ventured to Alaska by air after World War I. For the U.S. Army Air Service, there were many reasons to go.[6] Primarily, the Territory was strategically located as an important waypoint between North America and Asia. Operating military aircraft in extreme environments would test the airplane's practicality as a weapon, prove the ability of military aviation to reach distant territories in a short period of time, and showcase America's aeronautical industry. The notoriety from such flights would create popular support for the Air Service and its goal of becoming an independent air force within the U.S. military. Finally, the belief that the airplane was the key to progress in human civilization drove proponents of military aviation, like the rest of society, to embrace new ways to use it. Alaska was a perfect proving ground to test aviation.

The Alaskan Air Expedition was the first expression of Alaska's importance to American military aviation. Planners had three main goals. They wanted to pioneer a direct route to Asia that could be used in the event of war. Nome faced the Bering Strait, which divided North America and Asia. The extreme weather conditions and terrain encountered during the flight would be a great opportunity to assess the Air Service's new DH-4B biplanes. The DH-4B was an improved version of the service's standard two-seat observation and bomber airplane that featured strut-and-wire bracing, wood wings and the water-cooled 400-horsepower Liberty V-12 engine. Lastly, the expedition was to photograph unmapped areas of Alaska.

The four DH-4Bs, carrying eight officers and enlisted personnel, left Mitchel Field, Long Island, on July 25, 1920. They faced extreme weather and mechanical difficulties caused by rough landing fields as they worked their way across the upper Midwest and into Canada.

FAIRBANKS ALASKA, FIRST AIRPLANE IN ALASKA, LULY 19, 1920, 9452 A.S.

The Alaskan Flying Expedition landed at Exposition Park at Fairbanks on the afternoon of August 19, 1920. Capt. Street hand-delivered a copy of the New York Times he picked up when leaving Mitchel Field to the editor of the city newspaper, the Daily News Miner. Only seven years had passed since James and Lily Martin flew over the same ground, but the photographer hailed the arrival as a first for Alaska while getting the date wrong.

They added an unofficial responsibility when they collected mail packages for delivery at Nome. They first entered the Alaska territory at Wrangell where they made note of the countless glaciers. Over the Yukon, Streett noticed there were no open areas to land except for sand and gravel bars. From there, the Expedition flew to Fairbanks, continued on to Ruby, and reached Nome on August 23. They explored and photographed the surrounding area and landed where they could as the weather permitted before starting the return flight to New York on August 31. Streett and the Expedition reached Mitchel Field on October 20 having flown over 9,000 miles.

Upon his return, Streett recommended the airway to Alaska remain open since the airplane "provided a passage over country impassable by any other means."[7] To him, it was a matter of practicality for the Territory as well:

The people in the Alaskan settlements want aerial service, and a movement is under foot to inaugurate such service. When you consider that it costs from $55 to $65 a ton to transport freight from Seattle to Alaska, plus the charge for carrying it inland, you can see the possibilities of the airplane in reducing that cost.[8]

While Alaska was the destination for its first long-distance foray in 1920, the Air Service saw the Territory as an important waypoint for its next flight of spectacle: the first aerial circumnavigation of the

Members of the U.S. Army Air Service Alaskan Air Expedition. From left to right, Capt. St. Clair Streett and Lts. Clifford C. Nutt, Ross C. Kirkpatrick, Erik H. Nelson, and Clarence E. Crumrine. The flyers were also known as the "Black Wolf Squadron" due to the distinctive insignia painted on their DH-4B aircraft.

globe. The immediate goal of the U.S. Army Air Service World Flight was to evaluate the airplane as a global technology. Additionally, connecting the world by air routes would foster better international relations and encourage commerce. A successful flight would also generate international prestige for the United States.

On April 6, 1924, eight pilots and mechanics in four airplanes left Seattle, Washington. Named after American cities, the *Seattle*, *Chicago*, *Boston*, and *New Orleans* arrived at Resurrection Bay, Seward, Alaska, on April 14. Alaska became the crucial first test for the World Flight. The harsh Alaskan spring was one of the worst in decades. Heavy snows caused delay as the airplanes followed the coast northward. Lost in near-zero visibility, flight commander Maj. Frederick Martin and Sgt. Alva Harvey crashed the *Seattle* on a mountainside near Point Moller in southeastern Alaska, on April

30. Both survived, but their journey was over. The three remaining crews pushed on. When unable to fly, the crew slept in shacks with their beds made on boxes to keep the rats away. In the Aleutians, the fliers encountered williwaws, sudden, strong, destructive winds up to 75 miles per hour that rushed down from the mountains that threatened both them and their aircraft. On May 15, they left Attu on the first flight across the Pacific Ocean. The World Flight continued its journey west through Asia, the Middle East, and Europe. After losing the *Boston* in the North Atlantic, they reached Seattle on September 28. The World Flight's journey took 175 days later, seventy-four stops, and about 27,550 miles.

The Army continued to spread its wings toward Alaska during the summer of 1934. Aviation overall had undergone a technical and organization revolution in the ten years since the World Flight.

The Seattle, Chicago, Boston, and New Orleans of the U.S. Army Air Service World Flight appear over Resurrection Bay near Seward, Alaska, on April 13, 1924. Some of the local townspeople are watching from the tracks of the newly-operational Alaska Railroad.

The townspeople of Seward view three aircraft from the U.S. Army Air Service World Flight moored in Resurrection Bay. The rough terrain and lack of airfields meant the flight had to install floats on their World Cruisers to get through Alaska.

Each of the ten Army Air Corps B-10s that ventured northwest to Alaska in 1934 carried distinctive "nose art" insignia commemorating the flight. Besides Fairbanks, other cities and areas recognized were Anchorage, Kotzebue, and Denali.

Pursuing its dream of creating a fleet of intercontinental strategic bombers, the Army Air Corps purchased the new Martin B-10 bomber. Considered one of the first "modern" airplanes, the twin-engine monoplane featured all-metal construction, retractable landing gear, and an overall streamline design. Lt. Col. Henry H. Arnold led ten B-10s toward Alaska to prove the tactical practicability of sending air units to the Territory and to train his men in flying over remote and uninhabited terrain.

On July 19, they left Bolling Field, Washington, D.C., and arrived in Fairbanks five days later after covering 4,000 miles in 25 hours and 30 minutes flying time. Arnold received an honorary totem pole from the people of Alaska on behalf of the Air Corps. During their stay, the unit photographed 23,000 square miles of the Territory before returning to Bolling Field via the western United States on August 16.[9]

As the American military ventured into Alaska to promote itself and aviation in general, civilian aviation grew to facilitate more flights of spectacle that electrified a culture increasingly enamored with the aviation. During the interwar years, aerial explorers were drawn to conquer the poles with the same drive as in the pre-war era, except that now they traveled by air. Arctic explorers immediately recognized that the airship and the airplane were the means to reach and document areas inaccessible any other way. During the spring of 1926, Norwegian explorer Roald Amundsen led a team of fifteen adventurers on the first aerial crossing of the Arctic Ocean. Their transportation was the *Norge* ("Norway" in Norwegian and pronounced "Norg-eh"), a semi-rigid airship designed and piloted by Italian engineer Umberto Nobile. They left Spitsbergen, Norway, on May 11 headed toward Nome, Alaska, by way of the North Pole. They reached the area of the Pole the next day. In increasingly worsening

Secretary of War George H. Dern congratulates Lt. Col. Henry H. Arnold on the successful completion of the B-10 flight from Washington to Fairbanks in July 1934. To recognize the achievement, the people of Alaska presented to the Army Air Corps a totem pole and members of the flight received Husky puppies as gifts.

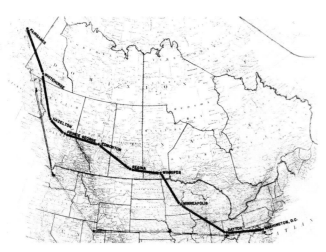

The route of the Army Air Corps B-10 flight to and from Alaska. Successfully flying to and from the Territory of Alaska demonstrated the long-range strategic potential of the Air Corps' bomber aircraft.

weather, they made a rough landing at the village of Teller, Alaska, seventy-five miles north of Nome, on May 14. The Alaska Natives equated the airship to a "great flying seal" as they saw it descend onto the ice of nearby Port Clarence. With the flight over, the Norge was to be dismantled and shipped to the United States.[10]

Australian polar explorer and pilot Hubert Wilkins wanted to be the first to fly over the top of the world in an airplane. He enlisted the assistance of a veteran Alaskan bush pilot, Carl Ben Eielson (1897–1929), and purchased a state-of-the-art high performance Lockheed Vega for the flight as part of the Detroit News-Wilkins Arctic Expedition. They left Point Barrow, the northernmost tip of Alaska, on April 15, 1928, and crossed the Arctic Sea. They landed near Spitsbergen twenty hours later. The 2,200-mile flight was a tremendous achievement in terms of endurance and skill and made

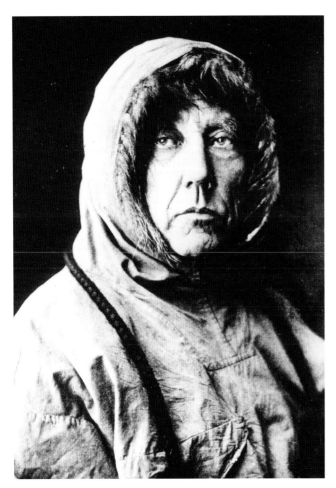

Norwegian explorer Roald Amundsen was well-known for his polar expeditions by the time the Norge left Spitsbergen for Nome in May 1926. This portrait, believed to be taken in Alaska around the time of the flight, features him in his Native-inspired Arctic anorak. Amundsen and five others disappeared two years later while flying to the Arctic to aid in the rescue of the crashed airship Italia.

The Norge, an Italian-built airship that carried out what many consider the first verified overflight of the North Pole on May 12, 1926. It was also the first aircraft to fly over the polar ice cap between Europe and America. The expedition was the brainchild of polar explorer and expedition leader Roald Amundsen, the airship's designer-pilot Umberto Nobile, and American explorer Lincoln Ellsworth. Here the airship lands at Teller, Alaska, where Alaska Natives referred to it as the "great flying seal."

the pair international celebrities, which included a knighthood for Wilkins. The successful flight across the Arctic, considered to be one of the greatest feats in aviation up to that time, yielded new information about the region and also cemented the fliers' reputation as skilled adventurers in the public eye.[11]

The airplane proved to be a useful tool for polar exploration, but there was a continuing goal in aviation to shorten the distance and time between far-flung parts of the globe. Aviators expressed this through multiple attempts to fly around the world as fast as possible. They chose the latest in aeronautical technology. Once again, Alaska served as an important byway and the climate and terrain proved to be a significant challenge.

Former Oklahoma wildcatter, Wiley Post (1898–1935) became a full-time pilot after losing his left eye in an oilfield accident. Post chose a Lockheed Vega, named Winnie Mae, and set out to break long-distance records. The one he wanted to shatter was around-the-world, which, since the Air Service World Flight's journey in 1924, had been reduced to twenty-one days by the airship Graf Zeppelin in August 1929. Post, Australian navigator Harold Gatty, and the Winnie Mae left New York on June 23, 1931. Five and a half days later, they faced one of the longest and most dangerous legs, a 2,500-mile flight from Siberia to Solomon, Alaska, near Nome. Crossing the Bering Sea, they encountered bad weather and were quickly running out of fuel. Fortuitously, they spotted Solomon and landed on a strip of beach to refuel. They were not so lucky at takeoff. The Winnie Mae tipped over in the soft sand, damaging the propeller and their chances of completing the journey. After making hasty repairs, they continued to Fairbanks and pushed on to Canada. They reached New York on July 1. Their entire journey was eight days, fifteen hours, and fifty-one minutes.

As part of the Detroit Arctic Expedition, Hubert Wilkins and Carl Ben Eielson used several aircraft during the polar expeditions. In the Fokker F.VIIA Alaskan, they took off on the first flight from Fairbanks to Barrow on March 31, 1926. They arrived in Barrow in a blizzard and set up two-way radio communication with Fairbanks, a first for the region. For the journey, Eielson flew while Wilkins navigated, which became the model for their 1928 Arctic crossing.

Refueling the Fokker Alaskan during the Detroit Arctic Expedition, with G.H. Wilkins as commander, 1926.

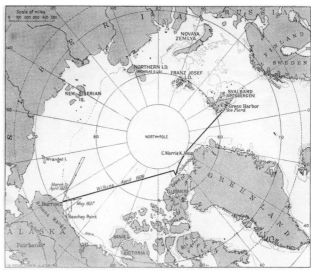

The route of Wilkins and Eielson's Arctic Ocean flight from Barrow to Spitsbergen.

Lost, tired, and frustrated with poor visibility, Wiley Post decided to land at the crude 700-foot airstrip at Flat, Alaska, on July 20, 1933. Unable to stop at the end, Post and the Winnie Mae crashed into a ditch, damaging the propeller and landing gear. Workers from the Flat Mining Company raised the Winnie Mae while Joe Crosson flew in a new propeller. Post was off the next morning headed toward Fairbanks.

Post wanted to build upon the success of his 1931 feat by flying around the world solo. He installed in *Winnie Mae* the latest navigational and performance technologies, which included an autopilot, automatic direction finder, and variable-pitch propeller. Post began at New York's Floyd Bennett Field on July 15, 1933, and flew east. Flying from Siberia, Post became lost in heavy clouds on July 20 and made an unscheduled landing at the small mining town of Flat, Alaska, which revealed he was 300 miles off of his original course to Fairbanks. Post damaged the *Winnie Mae* on the rough 700-foot strip. After making repairs, Post continued on to Fairbanks and reached New York on July 22. He had flown around the world in seven days, eighteen hours and forty-nine minutes.

Another pioneering aviator, Charles Lindbergh, along with his wife, Anne Morrow Lindbergh, came to Alaska in July 1931 to pursue new avenues for aviation. They flew their Lockheed Sirius monoplane equipped with floats over seemingly limitless expanses of uncharted and uninhabited territory as they flew to Point Barrow, Shishmaref, and Nome before venturing on to Soviet Siberia. Their journey "north to the Orient" was partly a vacation and partly an investigation into the practicability of international air lines using a great circle route – the shortest distance between two points on the globe – to reach Asia.

Wiley Post returned to Alaska in August 1935. He and his close friend and fellow Oklahoman, the famous American humorist Will Rogers, went on an aerial tour of the Territory. Post was interested in surveying possible airline routes to the Soviet Union and Rogers wanted new material for his weekly newspaper column. Rogers noted that their flight from Juneau to the famous Chilkoot Pass near Skagway took only ten minutes, a vast improvement over the two to three months time it took to travel the same distance overland.[12] After flying north, they became lost in bad weather and settled

On their way to Asia by way of the Arctic and North Pacific, Charles and Anne Lindbergh flew through Alaska in 1931. Besides investigating the Great Circle route, they interacted with Native peoples, all of which was recorded in Anne's book, North to the Orient (1935). Anne (seated in dog sled) and Charles (behind her), pose here with the villagers of Point Barrow.

down in a lagoon near Barrow on August 15. For the journey, Post combined the fuselage and wings of two different Lockheed aircraft to a pair of floats, which made the hybrid dangerously unbalanced. Shortly after takeoff, the engine failed and the uncontrollable Orion-Explorer floatplane crashed into lagoon killing both men instantly. Having survived on two previous occasions, Post was nevertheless unprepared for the challenge of flying in Alaska.

The 1938 around-the-world flight of Howard Hughes solidified Alaska's role as an important aerial byway. On July 10, 1938, Hughes and a crew of three left New York in a streamline Lockheed 14 airliner christened the *New York World's Fair* 1939. Unlike Post's forays to Alaska, the fuel stop in Fairbanks was systematic. They arrived back three days later having covered 14,824 miles in a whirlwind flight that symbolized the imminent arrival of the futuristic "World of Tomorrow" featured at the Fair. In the process, they proved that the airplane was

a global technology and that Alaska, at least for the United States, was an important stop along the way.

Some of the most important moments in aviation occurred in Alaska. As a byway, Alaska was the aerial bridge between North America, Asia, and Europe, which made it strategically located in terms of both military and commercial significance. Many aviators were just passing through as they sought to break records, extend the influence of their organizations, and express their enthusiasm for flight. Whether they stayed or went made no difference. Anyone flying in Alaska faced a challenge. While the use of this modern technology may have marked the end of the age of heroic exploration in many parts of the world, in the Arctic the situation was more complex. The Arctic was one of the last places still capable of testing both man and machine.

In this color tinted photograph (left to right), Will Rogers, famous Alaskan musher, Leonhard Seppala, Wiley Post, and Joe Crosson stand near Post's Lockheed monoplane on a floatplane dock on the Chena River near Fairbanks. Crosson advised Post to postpone the flight north into the Arctic until the Lockheed could be made safer and the weather improved. Anxious to get going, Post and Rogers pushed on toward Barrow.

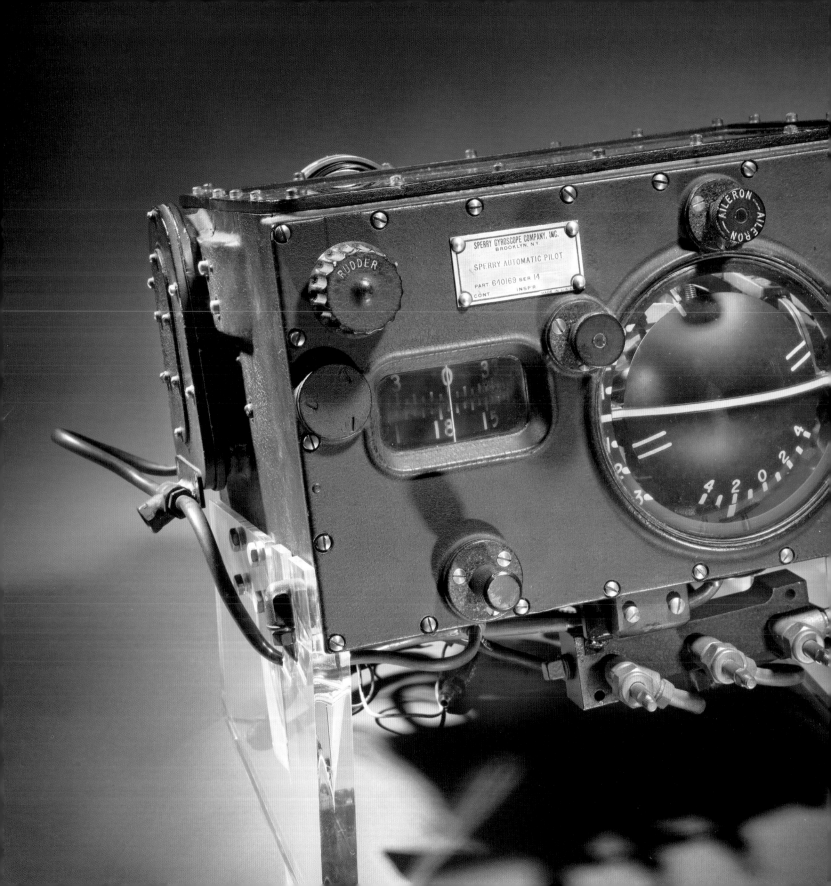

"Mechanical Mike" Automatic Pilot

Wiley Post's decision to fly around-the-world solo in 1933 meant he would have to fly and navigate at the same time. He chose a new innovation from the Sperry Gyroscope Company, an automatic pilot that could fly the Winnie Mae straight and level for long periods of time and distance by itself. Post used the device, nicknamed "Mechanical Mike", with navigational instruments to fly through continuous heavy clouds and fog during the long flight from Siberia to Fairbanks. He helped pioneer the type of all-weather flying needed to fly in Alaska.

Oil Cans, U.S. Army Air Corps

Ten U.S. Army Air Corps Martin B-10 bombers arrived in Fairbanks on July 24, 1934. They began their journey in Washington, D.C., to prove the strategic ability of the Air Corps. The inaccessibility of Alaska also meant that their successful flight was the result of a well-planned logistical effort. Modern air forces needed common supplies, such as the oil in these five gallon cans, to become the globe-ranging weapons their leaders and proponents envisioned.

Aero Club of America Aviation Medal of Merit
Capt. St. Clair Streett and his fellow pilots of the Alaskan Flying Expedition made one of the greatest flights in aviation. They received numerous honors and awards as they journeyed to and from Alaska over 9,000 miles. The Aero Club of America (today's National Aeronautic Association), the nation's premier aviation organization, bestowed upon them medals of merit upon their return. As the decades of the 1920s progressed, subsequent flights of spectacle overshadowed the expedition's achievement, which is largely forgotten in the early twenty-first century.

The Army Air Service World Flight embarked upon the first aerial circumnavigation of the globe in April 1924. Its four aircraft – Seattle (#1), Chicago (#2), Boston (#3), New Orleans (#4) – carried distinctive names, numbers, and insignia reflecting major American cities, their order in the flight, and their objective. After nearly a month in Alaska, the World Flight suffered the loss of the Seattle, the remains of which are preserved in the Alaska Aviation Heritage Museum in Anchorage. The fabric pictured here is from the Chicago, flown by Lts. Lowell Smith and Leslie Arnold, which took over as the lead ship in the World Flight. The restored Chicago can be seen in the Smithsonian National Air and Space Museum in Washington, D.C.

Heintz and Kaufman B1 Short-Wave Radio Transmitter
Australian explorer Hubert Wilkins and Alaskan bush pilot Carl Ben Eielson left Point Barrow, Alaska, for Spitsbergen, Norway, by way of the Arctic Ocean on April 15, 1928. During the twenty hour flight, Wilkins used this short-wave radio transmitter to send hourly reports back to Barrow, Alaska. Leon Vincent, the Barrow school teacher and radio operator, received them, but as the distance increased and the weather worsened, the messages became increasingly garbled. Wilkins and Eielson reached Norway, but a blizzard forced them to land and wait out the storm for five long days. Once the weather had cleared, they discovered they were just six miles from the settlement of Green Harbour near Spitsbergen.

Wiley Post-Will Rogers Crash Artifacts
Wiley Post was fatally unprepared to fly Will Rogers to Alaska in August 1935. His airplane featured a fuselage and wings from two separate Lockheed aircraft. Post, who had virtually no experience flying off the water, added Edo floats designed for a much heavier and larger Fokker trimotor airliner. Joe Crosson felt the airplane was nose-heavy and unsafe until further modifications could be made. Rogers, anxious to get going, urged Post to continue north to Barrow. This float access cap and earth inductor compass controller and generating unit were recovered from the wreckage of Post's crashed airplane near Barrow.

Shirt made from the dirigible Norge
In May 1926, bad weather caused the dirigible Norge to detour to Teller on its first flight over the North Pole from Norway to Nome. Upon landing, the dirigible collapsed. To make repairs, the crew removed the fabric cover and cast it aside. The airship was covered with three layers of fabric, each of a different material. The outer ply was a tough, silvery material, the second was of brownish oiled silk, and the inner layer was similar to very tightly woven linen. The Native villagers, who discovered the airship silk was an easy fabric to sew, were soon wearing garments made from the material. The brown was dark but could be lightened to the creamy yellow seen here when soaked in kerosene or vinegar.

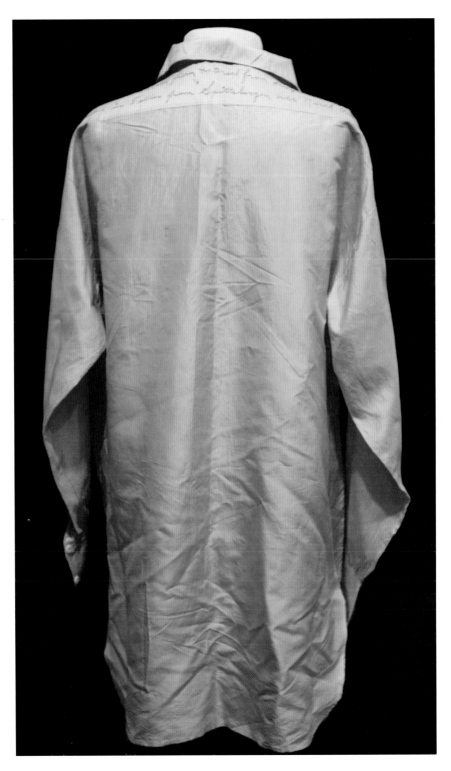

Earth Inductor Compass Generating Unit

Charles and Anne Morrow Lindbergh's unofficial trip to investigate the Great Circle route went through Alaska to Asia in 1931. Accurate and safe long-distance navigation was absolutely critical for flying in the Far North. Lindbergh chose an earth inductor compass, which measured the intensity of the earth's magnetic field to determine direction. Electromagnetic disturbances created by flying near the North Pole and the electrical system of their Sirius monoplane rendered a traditional magnetic compass unreliable. This General Electric Company generating unit, which extended from the fuselage of the Sirius, provided the needed electrical current for the compass.

TAKING TO THE AIR

TAKING TO THE AIR

The Martins' 1913 flight in Fairbanks did not kick off aviation in Alaska, at least not in the ways that would change life on the ground. It took another ten years for anyone in the Territory to think the airplane could offer more than spectacle. Before flying gained the public trust, "a thousand folks would come down to see the ship land and take off – but no one would get in it," pilot Cot Hayes recalled of his 1929 Seattle-to-Alaska air service.[13] When barnstormer Noel Wien (1899–1977) traveled to Alaska's interior in 1924, there were two working pilots. One of them, Carl Ben Eielson, believed that Alaska was a place where it was possible to make a living as a pilot. Eielson had been teaching school in Fairbanks in 1923 when some local businessmen put up money for a World War I-surplus Curtiss "Jenny" and allowed him to fly it around Fairbanks. Soon thereafter Eielson obtained a trial U.S.-mail contract and had a de Havilland DH-4B brought by

Noel Wien with the World War I Hisso Standard J-1, affectionately known as "Jenny," at Wiseman in the southern flanks of the Brooks Range in 1927. This was the first flight across the Arctic Circle in Alaska.

railroad to Fairbanks from the federal post office. He flew eight trips from Fairbanks to McGrath, a distance of about 280 miles, which constituted Alaska's first commercial flights. The route took twenty days to complete by dog sled teams, but Eielson flew it in four hours. After Eielson had three accidents, however, the post office deemed the experiment a failure. His contract was canceled, and he was told to return the airplane.

Wien, too, knew about being an unemployed pilot. He had jumped at an offer of $300 a month from Alaskan James "Jimmy" Rodebaugh (1887–1950) to fly for his company in Fairbanks.[14] Rodebaugh was a railroad conductor and the first promoter of the aviation business in Alaska, recognizing both a need for such services and the opportunity to make money. In the spring of 1924, Rodebaugh thus traveled to the Lower 48 to look for airplanes and pilots. He bought two Standards for $5,000, added extra fuel tanks, and replaced the anemic 90-horsepower Curtiss OX-5 engines with more powerful 150-horsepower Hispano-Suizas or "Hissos." For pilots Rodebaugh hired two farm boys, Noel Wien and Arthur Sampson, with little more than 500 hours of flight experience. With his airplanes and flyboys secured, Rodebaugh founded the Alaska Aerial Transportation Company (later renamed the Fairbanks Airplane Company).

While Wien's flying time was limited when he started working for the company, he quickly gained a reputation as a skilled though cautious pilot. To Rodebaugh's dismay, Wien would not fly in the winter regardless of the conditions, but in summer Wien was a pioneer – the first pilot in Alaska to cross the Arctic Circle, landing on the north side to transport two Fairbanks miners to their claim; the first to make a non-stop flight from Fairbanks to Anchorage; the first

POST OFFICE DEPARTMENT—FEBRUARY 12, 1916

ADVERTISEMENT

INVITING

Proposals for Carrying the Mails of the United States

ON THE WITHIN-NAMED ROUTES

BY AEROPLANE

From October 1, 1916 (or such subsequent date as the Department may order), to the end of the contract term (June 30, 1917, in Massachusetts, and June 30, 1918, in Alaska)

PROPOSALS RECEIVED UNTIL 4.30 P. M. MAY 12, 1916

A. S. BURLESON, POSTMASTER GENERAL

POST OFFICE DEPARTMENT, 1916

The Alaska Engineering Commission was the federal agency responsible for public works in the Territory, which included the Alaska Railroad. In late 1915, the Commission contacted the U.S. Post Office Department to inform it that Alaskan aeronautical interests were willing to operate an air mail service with the support of a government contract. The Post Office issued bids, but none materialized. Nevertheless, it was the first indication of the Post Office's interest in air mail and that Alaska would be a part of the overall program.

THE OLD

THE NEW

THE OLD AND NEW MAIL SERVICES IN ALASKA.

Airminded aviation enthusiasts cast the different ways to deliver the mail in Alaska as an issue of modernity in the 1920s. Here, the mushers, sleds, and dog teams represented the traditional, or "old" method of delivering the mail, while the DH-4 mail plane symbolized the "new" modern form of carrying the same amount of mail.

Carl Ben Eielson's short-lived air mail service from Fairbanks to McGrath from February to May of 1924 included a stop at the railroad town of Nenana. On March 12, Eielson landed the DH-4 mail plane on the nearby frozen Tanana River and postal employees exchanged mail bags. Within four minutes, Eielson was on his way to McGrath.

to make a commercial flight between Fairbanks and Nome; and the first to fly from Alaska to Siberia across the Arctic Circle. Charmed by these adventures, Wien convinced his brothers Ralph, Fritz, and Sig to join him in Alaska. The cockpit of Wien's Standard biplane could accommodate two passengers in the front seat – barely. Given the frigid temperatures, passengers needed to dress warmly. In 1925, the Fairbanks Airplane Company purchased a Dutch-built Fokker F.III, which could haul cargo or passengers in an enclosed cabin positioned under the wing while the pilot flew in the open forward cockpit, making it the first enclosed-cabin air service in Alaska. The Fokker's shock-absorber system, comprised of bungee cords, enabled it to land on bumpy and uneven landing strips, and the aircraft could also be equipped with floats or skis. When the Fokker arrived in Fairbanks, other pilots shied away from the large airplane, but Wien was intrigued. He operated the airplane for the next two winters before a fully enclosed cabin aircraft with an air-cooled engine, a Stinson SB-1 Detroiter, became available. In 1927, Ralph and Noel bought one of the Standards from Rodebaugh and started their

own airline called Wien Air Alaska. By 1929, Noel had successfully made the first round-trip flight between the United States and Asia. While Wien was pioneering commercial aviation, Eielson had not given up on the airplane. After piloting the first airplane across the Arctic Ocean with Australian explorer Hubert Wilkins in April 1928, he established Alaskan Airway, upon his return. Eielson and his mechanic Earl Borland died in a crash on November 9, 1929 in Siberia. They were attempting to evacuate furs and personnel from the *Nanuk*, a cargo vessel trapped in the ice off of North Cape (Mys Shmidta on today's maps), but not before making a significant statement about the future dominance of air transportation in Alaska.

During the first years of flying in that challenging region, official runways did not exist. In any locales other than Fairbanks, landings were made in the summer on river gravel bars or treeless hilltops above a village. Villagers sometimes attempted to clear the local scrub for runways, but usually the lengths were too short or had too many obstacles. Towns in treeless tundra areas, such as Nome and

Ada and Noel Wien standing in front of a Wien Alaska Airways of Nome Stinson Detroiter airplane.

Kotzebue, had fewer natural barriers, but runways still needed to accommodate aircraft on wheels, since the tundra was soft in the summer. Winter, when the ground was frozen, allowed for easier landings, especially for airplanes equipped with skis, but the short days offered little light by which to detect the frozen "runways."

When Alaskans wanted airplanes to land at larger towns, citizens banded together to clear a runway. In the spring of 1923, the residents of Anchorage, at the time a little railroad town, declared a public holiday so that the entire population could turn out with rakes, shovels, and scythes to clear an airstrip. The strip was later named Merrill Field in honor of ex-Navy flier Russ Merrill (1894–1929), who pioneered flying in the Anchorage area before his airplane was lost over Cook Inlet in 1929.

In the 1920s the most popular map used for flying was a dogsled trail map that showed the roadhouses where mushers could rest and feed their dogs. There was no communication technology at Alaskan airfields and no supporting equipment. Maps of Alaska, sketched by the Road Commission, were accurate enough but incomplete. Huge areas were marked as "unsurveyed." Of areas that were charted, "there was a mighty lot of difference between looking at things from the ground and the air," explains Noel Wien. "The only maps we had were made by men on the ground. When we looked down at the same scene from the air, we saw something very different." [15]

Pioneer bush pilot Sam O. White (1891–1976) described finding himself fifteen to twenty-five miles off course if he tried to fly by such a ground-plotted map. Landscape features were not always where the map claimed they would be. Magnetic compasses did not work well in the cold, and most would not hold a heading. With imperfect maps and useless compasses, for pilots unfamiliar with Alaska's geography the experience of getting lost was common. Therefore, comments White,

[…] we developed a system of flying drainages, and using the compass only when we had one that worked. This didn't mean that we followed rivers and creeks. Instead, for every place we wanted to go, we cut drainages at certain angles that corresponded with the place we wanted to reach. We worked on a trial-and-error basis until we had been over a route a few times, had straightened the kinks, and organized our landmarks. Then we could go to wherever we wanted as straight as a string. After we had followed a number of routes and memorized the angles and the landmarks, we had a map of Alaska pretty much in our heads.[16]

Early bush pilots such as White were instrumental in mapping and surveying Alaska. Much less intentionally, they also affected dramatically the Territory's development when the Alaska Road Commission began to reassess its plans to build roads across the region. Telegraph wires and undersea cables did connect the Territory with the rest of the United States. Shortly after acquisition of Alaska, the U.S. Army arrived and set up posts in various locations. In 1900, the U.S. Congress appropriated approximately $500,000 for the establishment of a communications network linking those posts to the bustling gold mining camps and ultimately to the United States. The core of the network was a 1,400-mile telegraph line between Nome to Eagle by way of Valdez laid out mile-by-mile by U.S. Army Signal Corps officers and men. An undersea cable from Sitka to Seattle provided direct communication with the United States. The resultant Washington-Alaska Military Cable and Telegraph System (the Alaska Communications System after 1936) allowed instantaneous communication to the outside world, but did not serve as the basis for a reliable transportation network that could bring goods in and out of the region.

Companies involved in navigation by water and rail were also working hard to position themselves as anchors of transportation. Alaskans in the interior had lobbied for a railroad, seeing it as the optimal solution for moving freight and supplies to isolated mining districts as well as promoting homesteading and agricultural growth, which then would lead to jobs and prosperity. The Second Organic Act passed in 1912 enabled U.S. President Warren G. Harding to appoint a commission to recommend the best routes to the interior of Alaska from its coastline. On March 12, 1914, bells and fire alarms rang throughout Fairbanks to signal passage of the Alaska Railroad Bill. The legislation provided full government funding for construction of a railroad connecting Seward with Fairbanks. Harding traveled to Fairbanks to dedicate the Alaska Railroad in 1923, yet, at the same time as Harding was driving a symbolic golden spike into the rail, former schoolteacher Ben Eielson was flying overhead, signaling what would really transform Alaska's future. The 470-mile-long Alaska Railroad traversed ground so hazardous that it was common for the locomotive to jump its track, and in winter there were delays of hours and sometimes days while avalanches of snow were cleared from the track. By way of comparison, flying took a tenth of the time.[17]

The work of pioneering pilots such as Eielson and Wien demonstrated the competitive value of aviation in Alaska. Other bush pilots soon joined them, and airplanes began to replace overland freight and mail carriers, such as the dogsled, and even challenged the hegemonic power of the railroad. Mail, food, medical supplies, mining equipment, and passengers could be delivered quickly to remote camps, river bars, and towns. Air transportation caught on quickly. Residents in Alaska's hinterland were no longer dependent upon ground routes for connection with regional centers. Airplanes broke the isolation of communities previously accessible only by boat in summer or by dog team in winter.

Enhancing the success of air travel in Alaska was the fact that passenger fares were not prohibitive. It was actually the least expensive mode of transportation at the time. Travel by dog team, the only winter alternative, was at least as expensive, with the added costs of roadhouse lodging for perhaps two or three weeks. Furthermore, in terms of passenger comfort, flying in an open cockpit was not much different than riding in a dogsled in the numbing cold. Summertime travelers could go by boat, but the transit time involved weeks compared to hours in an airplane. Air travel also helped miners and trappers to extend their short working season. Alaskans thus grasped the airplane's convenience for passenger transportation immediately.

However, as with Eielson's loss of his airmail route to the tried-and-true dogsled method, the airplane was not the obvious or immediate winner in its competition with dogs for the delivery of goods. It took some time for the airplane to prove its worth. Pilots were quick converts, some of whom had previously delivered goods by dogs. White, for example, who had worked as a warden for the Alaska Game Commission both by dog team and airplane, observed:

I was troubled having to depend on a team of freethinking dogs for transportation. A dog team is an inefficient mode of travel. It was kind of silly in a way. Most of my time was taken up taking care of the dogs, feeding them, exercising them, training them, instead of the important and constructive activity of enforcing game laws. A

good part of my annual expense allotment, usually around $2,500, supposedly for travel, went down their throats.

For earlier years, of course, it was about the only possible method of winter travel in the interior, other than shanks mare [or one's own legs]. But now there was an alternative – the airplane. When I saw what an airplane could do, I realized that the only way the Game Commission was going to get anywhere enforcing wildlife laws in Alaska was by taking to [the] air. I didn't know how to fly, but since others could fly, I figured I could learn to do it, too. It turned out that I figured right."[18]

As the airplane slowly edged ahead of the dogsled, bush flying became a permanent feature in Alaska. A relatively modest sum of money sufficed for purchase of a surplus military aircraft such as the Jenny or Standard, but maintenance was an issue. Besides being self-taught mechanics, early bush pilots also had to be willing to take any kind of load to any runway on or off the map and know the limits of their aircraft as well as the financial resources of their customers. Flying in challenging weather conditions with inadequate radio communication, heavy loads, and limited cash flow was not an easy life and entailed a number of risks. An airplane stranded on a stretch of frozen tundra or a remote lake left its pilot with few options. The pilot could fix the problem or perish. Bush pilots consequently learned to trade out an engine in the darkness of winter, repair collapsed landing gear with limited tools, and replace frozen fluids in the middle of an artic nowhere.

Pioneering bush pilots even declared their prowess and purpose in comparison with established international carriers such as Pan

The personal service that was a watchword with Wien was evident in 1925 when Noel Wien made the first commercial flight between Fairbanks and Nome. Here Fairbanks Mayor Dr. F. Dela Vernge (in derby) hands Noel a letter for personal delivery in the Bering Sea city some 560 miles distant. The Fokker monoplane left Fairbanks June 5, 1925 and made the flight in 7 hours and 40 minutes. Cost of that first charter was $1,500.00.

American Airways, or Pan Am, which offered flights to and throughout Alaska. When Harold Gillam (1902–1943) took over Pan Am's mail run from Fairbanks to Bethel in 1938, he established a previously unheard-of record of 100 percent completed schedules. Pan Am had flown the route "sensibly," waiting out good or, as it came to be known, "Pan Am weather." "We could set our watch by dog teams," complained customers in the twenty-odd scattered villages along the 500-mile route, "but no one knows when the airplanes are coming." However, when Gillam took over Pan Am, they could know to the minute, regardless of the weather that often threatened success. Other pilots began referring to storms as "Gillam weather."[19]

Such weather reports, though, were not easy to come by. The Alaska Communications System, under the Army Signal Corps, helped pilots by offering daily updates on weather from its few stations. "They looked out their window and made a report and a forecast at 8:00 a.m. and 1:00 p.m.," said bush pilot Cot Hayes. "Between and after, it was anybody's guess."[20]

Pilots were forced to memorize Alaskan rivers, lakes, mountains, flats, and their relationship to each other. Noel Wien said that he relied upon an inborn sense of north versus south that never failed him. Usually, when lost, he was able to find a topographical feature from which he could track his way to safety. If all else failed, he learned to fly downriver and hope that little rivers would lead to larger rivers, along which he might find a cabin.

While the sameness of the interior's summer terrain was problematic to pilots using the ground to navigate, the pervading white of winter was far worse. Wien taught himself to pick out details amid the whiteness: stumpy willows edged with white must be a stretch of the Chena River; a different reflection of light indicated a road on which snow had been packed by wagon wheels. "I was often tired from flying," Wien said. "I never flew relaxed or daydreamed, but was continually looking for possible landing spots. Where would I land now? […] I [always] was looking, looking, looking."[21]

"Contact navigation" designates the situation when an aviator gets from here to there by looking at the ground and picking up anticipated checkpoints. Whereas pilots in the more southern states looked for parks, golf courses, church steeples, and cities, bush pilots in the remoteness of the North had none of these landmarks. Instead, there were thousands of lakes, ponds, rivers, and mountains that looked identical. Features such as a lake, river, dog trail, or roadhouse looked like so many other clusters that an Alaskan bush pilot could be thrown off by many miles. "You had to learn to drag a possible landing spot at the lowest possible altitude," Wien said about such airfields. "A spot could look much different from five feet up than from twenty-five. The throttle was on the right, so I'd look out the left while making an approach, but on strange bars I'd twist from side to side to watch for gullies, driftwood, holes, and rocks."[22]

Flying against the elements without the aid of informational resources created the legacy and lore of the Arctic bush pilot. The term itself, "bush pilot," evokes the golden age of aviation – cowboy pilots skillfully maneuvering a vintage aircraft into the most inhospitable regions on earth. The romantic images were perpetuated by popular culture. When the Junior Birdmen of America, a national boys club in the 1930s, conducted an annual popularity poll in newspapers to vote for favorite pilots, Alaskan bush pilot Joe Crosson (1903–1949) was featured alongside Eddie Rickenbacker, Charles Lindbergh, Amelia Earhart, Jimmy Doolittle, and Howard Hughes.[23]

Crosson was also featured on the CBS network radio show called *Sky Blazers: True Adventures of Heroes of the Air,* and hosted by Roscoe Turner, a famous air racing pilot and aviation personality. *True Comics* in 1941 included stories about American General George C. Marshall, the American flag, First Lady Dolly Madison, Nationalist Chinese General Chiang Kai-shek, and Joe Crosson. He was also a featured aviator in a series of stamps produced by Skelly Oil as a sales promotion. Among the other fliers depicted on the stamps were Amelia Earhart, Wiley Post, and Jimmy Doolittle. After Crosson appeared in a Camel cigarette advertisement, the company continued to send him a carton of cigarettes each month for years.[24]

While the romance surrounding it is subjective, bush flying is one of the last vestiges of aviation's early roots and is still relied upon by many isolated communities to provide a vital lifeline. Alaska, the barren northern territories of Canada, and Australia are the locales most commonly associated with bush flying, although its impact extends equally to the rainforests of South America and the jungles of Africa.

In the small villages scattered across Alaska, bush pilots became larger-than-life figures. Growing up in Haycock, a small Alaskan mining town near Nome in western Alaska, Inupiat Holger "Jorgy" Jorgensen (1927–), who later became a bush pilot and airline captain, remembered the first airplane coming into his village when he was six years old:

The mining companies had completed this little airport in 1933. They built the runway with horses and by using a steam shovel and putting a deadman down to move the dirt back and forth. They finally got a runway built that was about 800 feet long. […] The pilot of that first airplane was Noel Wien. All of us young kids and everybody else, even the old miners, paid more attention to what he was wearing than what the airplane looked like. I think it was an open-cockpit airplane up front, and it had a little cabin in the back. But what I do remember is what the pilot looked like. He had a leather outfit on – a leather jacket, a leather hat with a pair of goggles, leather riding boots, a pair of leather mittens, a wool scarf, and riding britches made of 100 percent wool. And I wanted to look like that. Nearly all of the kids there that I grew up with, both a little bit older than me and a little bit younger, just about all of them went on to learn how to fly. Everybody back then got the bug after seeing that first airplane coming in there and looking at the pilot and the way he was dressed. You would have thought that it was God that came out of the air and landed. Many […] just swarmed this guy by the name of Noel Wien.[25]

Bush pilots served as the grocery store, mailmen, mail-order catalogue, ambulance, and communication network for a village. Their diverse cargo included mining equipment, food, and personal items from families and friends elsewhere. While bush piloting attracted independent and sometimes gruff personalities, the pilots, for the most part, overcame their social reluctance and recognized their public role. Sam White flew mail for Noel Wien and learned to enjoy making the daily runs:

I bumped into old friends everywhere I went, and I liked visiting with them as well as providing them with a needed service. I spent my days flying, and my evenings shopping for everything from pins and diapers to light plants, axes, and saws for the people in the sticks. And woe to the pilot who forgot the nipples for the baby's bottle. Villagers had two weeks between scheduled flights to write their orders, but they never got around to it. They were always caught by surprise when the mail plane arrived, resulting in half a dozen folk at a time shouting verbal orders, and thrusting loose money at me. I had to have a portable accounting outfit in my pocket and "make book" even at forty-five degrees below.[26]

While often associated with bravery and heroism, the bush pilot's life was not glamorous in its day-to-day demands. This was practical, hard work, and often dangerous, requiring specialized knowledge and skill. Born with a scrappy mentality, bush pilots exuded the traits they needed to survive, and it was the airplane that created that character. Such pilots were drawn to a world that allowed them to be their own boss and make their own decisions in a place where few had traveled. But they also were in a profession that served people, and so their cockiness was balanced by discretion.

The most notable pilots were not brash when it came to flying. While there was, and still is, a pressure to fly in all weather, how often bush pilots chose not to fly was an important indicator of their prudence. They knew that survival meant flying smart and that no machine could conquer the Arctic elements that demanded their respect.

While all skilled bush pilots developed their own sense of reading weather and terrain through experience in the air, Native Alaskan pilots were able to use their distinct sense of the landscape as a valuable tool in navigation. These indigenous Alaskans adapted to the airplane with enthusiasm. Jorgy recalled the magnetism of his first flight:

I first rode in a plane at age twelve. A few of us, George Johnson, who sat up in front, and David Jonson, who sat on a gas box with me in the back, each paid Sig Wien five dollars to take us up. I could watch him do everything. We all knew right then and there that this was what we wanted to do. It was very exciting because of the feel of the airplane. It felt so good […] the feel of the air. When my mother found out I gave five bucks for that ride she hollered, "Are you crazy?" She was very upset.[27]

Jorgy first met Sig Wien when the latter started flying into the Haycock mining camp from Nome. Upon spotting the airplane, the boy was usually the first one to greet Wien. When Jorgy was thirteen, Wien allowed him to drive some of the mail with his dog team from Haycock to Koyuk, a distance of about twenty-one miles, in the winter, but it was the airplane that fascinated Jorgy. Finally, one day at the mining camp, Sig asked Jorgy if he would like to go to Nome and take care of his airplane for him – load it up, heat it in the morning, and get it ready for departure – and Jorgy's lifelong connection to the airplane was cemented.[28] Others encouraged him along the way:

There were a lot of guys that really bugged me to learn how to fly, and one was a guy by the name of Burt Beltz. He was from the

In 1979, Ellen Paneok became the first Alaska Native woman to earn a pilot's license. She accumulated 15,000 hours over the course of her career bush flying in Alaska. Paneok's Inupiaq Native elders called her "Owl Eyes" due to her ability to see and fly in weather that many pilots could not. Besides flying and writing for popular magazines, she cultivated an interest in the restoration of classic bush planes flown by the pioneers, which included the Stinson Gullwing. Photograph by Carolyn Russo.

same mining camp that I'm from. He was older than me but he had learned how to fly, and he kept bugging me to learn. He influenced me a lot, and he was also half-Native. I think he got his start flying in about 1940. Then there was Herb Nichelson. I got acquainted with him, and he had a brother by the name of Elmer Nichelson.

There were half-Native guys, and they started flying out of Dillingham in the later 30s and the first part of the '40s, and I ran across both of them when I was in the service and they were flying out of Bethel. Then I ran across another Native pilot down there by the name of Bob Vanderpool. He was starting up this little flying business out of Red Devil, but he would come into Bethel quite a bit when I was in the service there. And there was another guy by the name of Eddie Hanson, and he had only one eye. He was a half-Native guy from King Salmon. He influenced me a lot. A lot

of people looked up to him and to all the other Native pilots that I met during that time. I think they are all gone now.[29]

In 1943, when Jorgy was sixteen years old, he took his first flying lessons from Frank Whaley, who had started a flight school in Nome called Rainbow Flying Service. "My instruction was going to be in an Air knocker. That was a little Aeronca three-cylinder airplane, and I think it was roughly 38 horsepower. But they could never get it to run," recalled Jorgy.

Then in 1944, they brought in a little 65-horse J-5 Cub. It was a three-place, a little Continental, and he hired a young lady to come over and run the little flight school. Her name was Pearl Laska, and she was about twenty-six or twenty-seven years old. […] She had quite a few students. As far as I could get was just up to getting a solo ticket from *her because I had to get authorization from my mother before I could solo. My mother was deathly against me learning how to fly, and she took every chance she'd get to run it down. [...] So my older sister signed it for me.*[30]

Jorgy is one of many Native Alaskans who flew, and still fly, over Alaska as a bush pilot. Ellen Paneok (1959–2008), who was born in Kotzebue and raised in a foster home in Anchorage, was one such skilled pilot. In her mid-teens she read a magazine article on aviation careers and decided to take flying lessons. At age sixteen she began to fly, paying for lessons with her income from making scrimshaw. Eventually she became a commercial pilot, owning ten different aircraft throughout her career, flying the bush, and landing on islands, lagoons, sandbars, icepacks, gravel pits, and mountain airstrips. Another early Native Alaskan bush pilot was William English, who was born in Wiseman in 1923 as the son of an Inupiat mother and a Caucasian father. English was one of several Native Alaskans to work with Wien Airlines.

Eventually there were enough pilots in Alaska to ensure competition for air service. When passenger boats (the only means of getting from Alaska to the States) came up the inside passage to Valdez and Seward, pilots swarmed the docks in search of travelers seeking inland transportation to their home bases. Hans Mirrow picked up passengers headed for Nome, Oscar Winchell corralled those going to Anchorage, Noel Wien took people traveling to Fairbanks, and Bob Ellis vied with Alex Holden for passengers to Juneau, Ketchikan, and Sitka in southeastern Alaska, where there was not enough flat land for a railroad, highway, or even airstrip but where a float plane could slip in easily. [31]

Bush pilots consequently became known for the particular area they served and for their flying techniques. Bob Reeve (1902–1980), for example, was recognized as the "glacier pilot" for his work in serving the mining community near Valdez and for his ingenious methods of landing on mountainside snow and ice. Bradford Washburn, himself a pilot who had worked with French, Canadian, and Alaskan pilots, said in an interview that Reeve was "without doubt the finest ski pilot and rough-country flier I have ever seen."[32] Polar explorer Admiral Richard Byrd issued a statement to the press in 1937 that Reeve had broken the world's record for the highest landing on skis, which was over 1,800 feet higher than any previous elevation in either Arctic or Antarctic expeditions.

It was in Reeve's financial interest to find a way to service the mines in both summer and winter, but in winter, when he could make a ski landing, the lodes were covered with snow, and he could not find them. In summer, when they were visible, he was on wheels and could not land. He therefore was determined to figure out how to take off from Valdez with skis in the summer so that he could set his aircraft and freight on the mountain with the necessary landing gear. Studying the possibilities, Reeve discovered an area two miles west of town, part of Valdez Bay, which was covered by tidewater, but between tides it offered a slick surface of fine clay silt and wet grass. Except for the problem of nightly tides, he felt that it would provide a good medium for ski take-offs and landings. "While other pilots were operating by clock and calendar," said Reeve, "I began using a tide book for a manual of operations."[33] The mudflat flying was a spectacle for Valdez and it attracted tourists. "If I could have charged admission," said Reeve, "I really would have had it made."[34]

It was Joe Crosson who pioneered the slopes of Mount McKinley by airplane, blazing the way for others. On clear days Mount McKinley, also known as Denali ("the Great One" in the Athabaskan language), towers high above the surrounding landscape. In the 1930s, Crosson flew tourists, businessmen, and governors to the mountain, but his Fairchild 71 monoplane remained airborne rather than landing on the mountain's slopes. He also led flights to determine the mountain's elevation above sea level because no accurate measurements had been made. Crosson's airplane carried four different altimeters. The event was recorded on film for release on newsreels throughout

Bob Reeve in his Fairchild 51 on the Columbia Glacier landing field, supplying the Ruff & Tuff mine outside of Valdez, 1938. Parts of a new diesel engine are unloaded in the foreground.

the nation. Crosson's observations and the results from scientific instruments showed that the summit was slightly above 20,000 feet (it is now measured at 20,320 feet).

In the spring of 1932, Mount McKinley was the focus of two expeditions. Mountaineer and scientist Allen Carpe, who was leading a climbing party with the goal of using the mountain's elevation as a platform for a study of cosmic rays, led one. He hired Crosson to help him establish camp on the Muldrow Glacier, using the airplane to move his team and their supplies as close to the mountain as possible. The slopes of McKinley presented unique challenges to pilots because there were no trees or structures on the glacier to provide an indication of distance or scale. Boulders that were visible could have been five feet high or fifty. On April 25, Crosson guided his Fairchild in for a perfect landing at an elevation of about 5,600 feet, introducing high-altitude mountain flying to Denali. One of the climbing-team members noted that Crosson took the landing "much as a matter of course, and lit a cigar before leaving the plane."[35]

Mount McKinley inspired later aeronautical efforts as well. In the 1950s, Bradford Washburn – explorer, mountaineer, photographer, and cartographer – was determined to survey Mount McKinley. While he was adept at trekking and climbing, he knew that it would be far more productive to start out on the mountain than to have to hike to it. He eventually recruited bush pilot Don Sheldon (1921–1975) to help him. On the day of his first flight with Sheldon in 1951, Washburn went to Anchorage to visit his old friend Bob Reeve, who told Washburn: "I've heard a lot about that kid [Sheldon], and he's either crazy and is going to kill himself, or he'll turn out to be one hell of a good pilot!"[36]

Washburn paid Sheldon $25 an hour as a charter rate but $50 for a new-area landing on the mountain. Seeing the possibility of future work, Sheldon quickly became an expert at accomplishing glacier landings and pioneered aviation on the mountain. With typical understatement Sheldon described his first glacier landing:

Hell, it was no big thing. I already knew that you had to look the area over before you landed, and had to do it in good light. The landing area had to be steep enough to slow you down as you landed uphill and assist you when you took off downslope. It had to be smooth enough to keep you out of the crevasses and offer enough room for an overrun. After that, I just went ahead and did it.[37]

Of course, glacier landings are some of the most delicate and skilled of maneuvers. Sheldon and pilots who followed him to the mountain learned to read shadows, which could indicate a drifted surface and, more importantly, show subtle indentations hinting at crevasses – some big enough to engulf a tiny Super Cub. The snow that covers these crevasses is sometimes only a few inches thick, and even one mistake would be deadly for a pilot and his passengers. As noted by bush pilot Pete Haggland, "Even routine landings that he [Sheldon] makes would raise hair on a frozen orange."[38]

By the end of the 1930s, there were over 100 airfields in Alaska. Modern aircraft of the time were only suited for those in Anchorage,

Don Sheldon at Mt. McKinley with his Piper, 1955.

Harold Gillam in his open cockpit biplane wearing heavy fur clothing to withstand the Arctic weather.

This plane on skis (c. 1930s) demonstrates the ability of early bush planes and pilots to haul cargo, even in winter. This load includes Magic Baking Powder, yeast, Fort Garry Tea, and Ivory soap. These planes and their pilots were the main source of supplies for the Native villages across Alaska.

Fairbanks, Juneau, and Nome. Less than 200 commercial aircraft flew several tons of freight and covered millions of miles. In 1938, Alaskan aviation became subject to federal control. The Depression-era Civil Aeronautics Act created a Civil Aeronautics Authority (CAA) to regulate air traffic in the interest of a healthy business model. Commercial airlines could serve only those communities for which they were certified. To become certified, an airline had to prove that it had provided continuous and adequate service between one community and another from May to August of 1938. Government regulation of the highly individualized bush-pilot operations was a blow to Alaskan pilots. Many small air services were either forced out of business or had to consolidate with other companies. For years Alaskan flight operators had been bidding on annual mail contracts and losing money on them. By 1939, about the only ones to bid on

the mail contracts were those who were far-sighted enough, such as Harold Gillam, to anticipate what the Civil Aeronautics Act of 1938 might actually bring about.

Aviation was growing in Alaska far more rapidly than in other parts of the United States due mainly to the lack of ground transportation. Alaska airplanes were providing enough mail service for Alaska's 60,000 residents to equal the service provided to close to three million in the states so it seemed reasonable that Alaska was entitled to a healthy share of the money spent for air-navigation aids, airfield construction, and airmail service. In order to give Alaskan carriers the benefits of CAA legislation, Civil Aeronautics Board inspectors had to have accurate accounts from the airlines to determine whether their businesses were being run efficiently and whether they were

Pacific Alaska Airways initiated regular air mail and passenger service from the lower forty-eight states to Alaska on June 20, 1940. The four-engine Sikorsky S-42 *Alaskan Clipper* flew the Seattle-Ketchikan-Juneau portion while a Lockheed Electra continued the route on to Fairbanks and Nome. The airline issued this first-day mail cover to celebrate the "Pan-Pacific First Flight". Louis Gilman mailed one to himself as a memento of the flight.

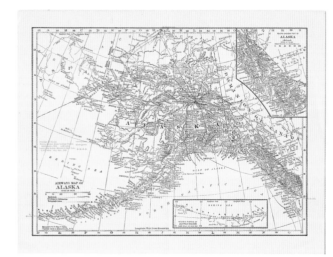

By 1929, Alaska had its own network of airways that not only connected the far-flung settlements of the Territory together, but indicated its importance as a global aerial byway as well.

Harold Gillam stands beside a Stearman on skis. In 1929, Ben Eielson purchased this single-engine biplane Stearman from Noel Wien for the newly established Alaskan Airways, Inc. In November 1929, pilot Eielson and his mechanic, Earl Borland, were lost while flying a Hamilton Metalplane to Siberia in an attempt to assist the stranded fur ship, Nanuk. With only 40 hours flight time, novice aviator Harold Gillam flew the Stearman on an extraordinary search for the downed men. The plane was among the first to land on Mount McKinley in 1932, and also made historic flights to Arctic villages with diphtheria serum in 1931 with pilot Joe Crosson.

Two men refuel a Pacific Alaska Airways Lockheed Model 5B Vega floatplane moored at a dock somewhere in Southeast Alaska in the 1930s.

entitled to government subsidies in the form of mail pay. But the bush pilots' systems of accounting proved a little less than adequate by government standards. The Civil Aeronautics Board came to Alaska to regulate commercial flying, allot routes, and fix rates. In October 1942, temporary certificates were issued to Alaskan carriers. Subsidies, in the form of mail rates, were not established for Alaskan pilots for another five years. In all it took nine years for Alaska's bush pilots to receive the benefits of the protective legislation that carriers in the states enjoyed. And it was to be another nine years before they were granted permanent certificates.[39]

Aircraft charter rates were $40 to $80 for a six-place airplane or an average passenger rate per mile of 18 to 20 cents. Typical freight rates were $1.10 to $2.04 per pound. Air travel was relatively expensive. The $68 airfare from Anchorage to Naknek 300 miles away was as much as the Seattle-Seward-Anchorage boat and train fare. In the first eight months of 1939, air-carrier revenue in Alaska amounted to nearly $900,000; 60 per cent of this was on credit.[40]

In addition to regulation, the CAA began a program of constructing airfields. By January 1940, Alaska had ten airfields with runways of 2,500 feet or more. Alaska was allowed to participate in the Federal Aid Airport Program in 1940, which provided federal subsidies for airport construction. The Territorial Legislature passed an aviation fuel tax to provide the Territory's share of the construction program. Pan Am's subsidiary Pacific Alaska Airways started Seattle-to-Alaska service in 1940. Congress authorized federal funds for major "continental category" airport construction at Anchorage and Fairbanks. Despite such rapid development, aviation in Alaska was still widely conducted on gravel, glacier, and sand with small airplanes and localized networks.

Dog Sled and Mail Bags
The U.S. Mail traveled in Alaska first by dogsled, the traditional and most celebrated form of overland travel in the region. In the 1920s, bush pilots and their airplanes competed with mushers and their dog teams and sleds to be the dominant and desired means of transportation. Each method ebbed and flowed in dominance over the following decades with the airplane gaining prominence after World War II.

Rotating Airport Beacon, Fairbanks Federal Building
Fairbanks served as the center of aviation during the early years of flight in Alaska. Opened in 1923, Weeks Field was where the early pioneers pursued opportunities in the air. As aviation continued to grow in the region in the mid-1930s, this beacon, perched atop the nearby Federal Building in downtown Fairbanks, provided the location of the field to pilots flying at night and in bad weather. Weeks Field closed with the opening of the Fairbanks International Airport in 1951.

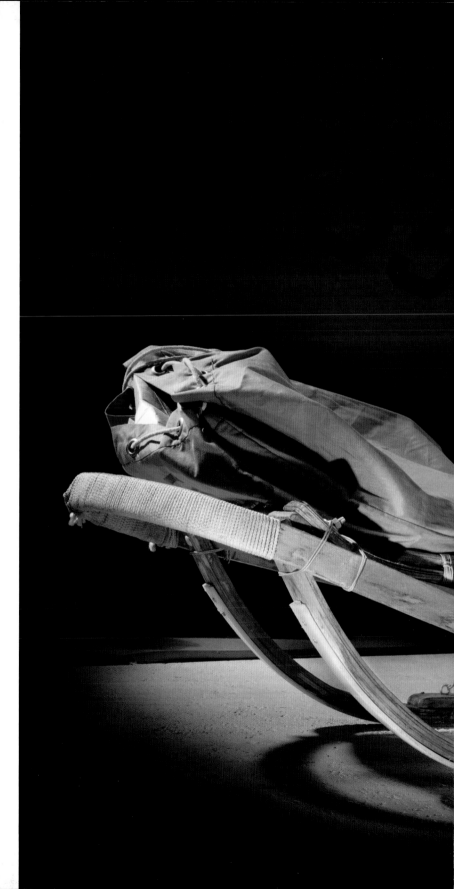

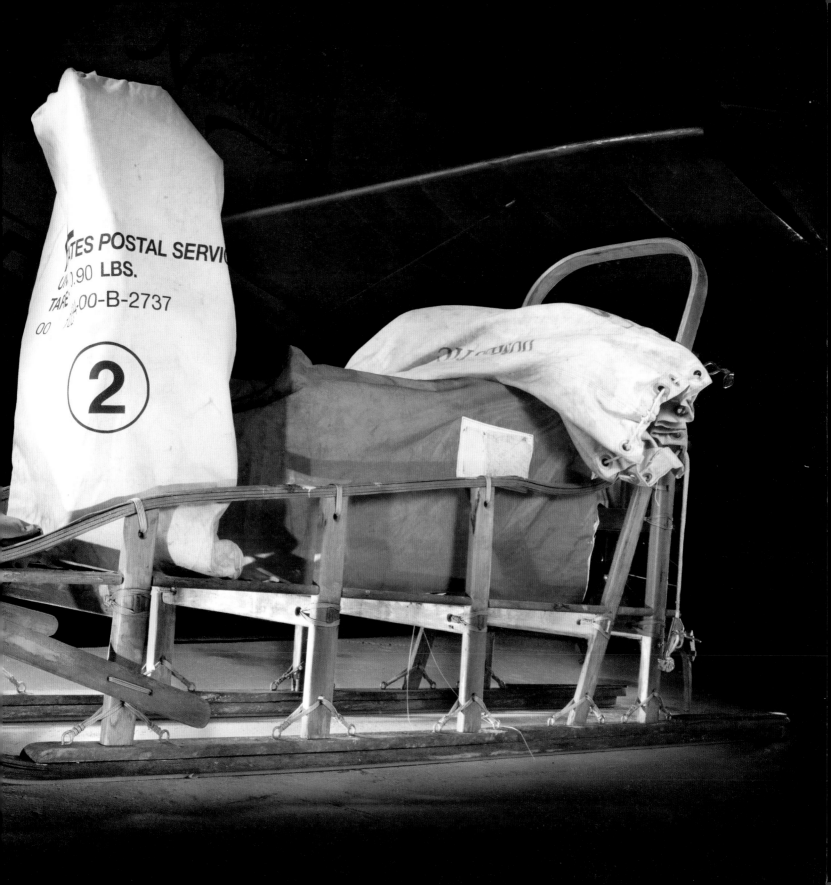

James Kivetoruk Moses. Mail Dog Carrier going through Camp, 1962.

Depiction of early U.S. mail delivery by dog sled in Nome, Alaska. The primary communication and transportation link to the rest of the world during the summer was the steamship; but between October and June the northern ports like Nome became icebound, and dog sleds delivered mail, firewood, mining equipment, gold ore, food, furs, and other needed supplies between the trading posts and settlements across the interior and along the western coast. Roadhouses where travelers could spend the night sprang up every 14 to 30 miles until the end of the 1920s, when the mail carriers were replaced by bush pilots flying small aircraft and the roadhouses vanished. Dog sledding persisted in the rural parts of Alaska, but was almost driven into extinction by the spread of snow machines in the 1960s.

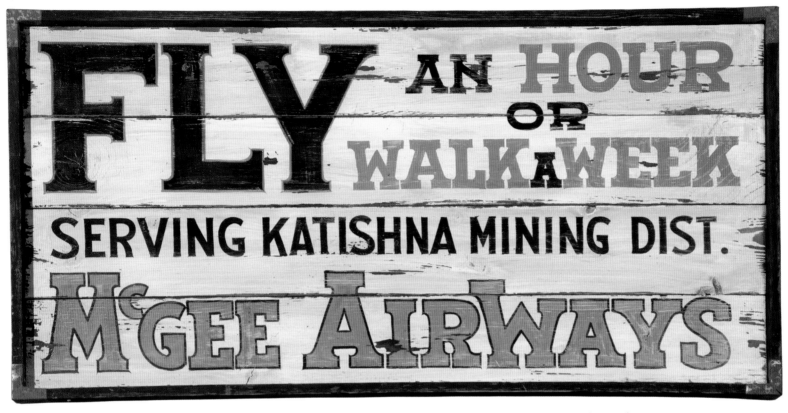

McGee Airways Sign
Linious "Mac" McGee founded McGee Airways in 1932, making it one of the first air services in Anchorage. After establishing air mail, charter, and cargo service across southwestern and central Alaska, McGee Airways merged with competitor Star Air Service in 1934. McGee managed Star at crucial times and made it a successful operation before retiring from aviation in 1937. Star renamed itself Alaska Airlines in 1944.

Luggage Cart, Weeks Field
Pan American Airways established its subsidiary, Pacific Alaska Airways, in 1932 to provide commercial service connecting the major cities of the territory. To better connect Alaska to the lower forty-eight states, Pacific Alaska started a route connecting Seattle, Juneau, Fairbanks, and Nome with Lockheed Electra airliners in 1940. Porters at Weeks Field used this luggage cart to assist passengers as they departed from or arrived in Fairbanks. Pan American absorbed Pacific Alaska into its regular operations in 1941.

Aluminum Skin Fragment, Hamilton Metalplane
In 1929, Carl Ben Eielson was an aviation celebrity well-known on the world stage for his Arctic and Antarctic flights. On November 9, Eielson and his mechanic, Earl Borland, crashed off the coast of Siberia while rescuing the passengers and cargo of the ice-bound ship Nanuk. An extensive international search for Eielson and Borland discovered their bodies and their airplane seventy-seven days later. A member of the search party, Jim Hutchison, cut this piece of the fuselage skin from Eielson's Hamilton Metalplane as a personal memento.

Pilot's license of Russel ("Russ") Hyde Merrill
Merrill was an Alaskan aviation pioneer. Born in
Des Moines, Iowa, he became a U.S. Navy pilot
during World War I, becoming Naval Aviator No.
469. After the war, he received a chemistry degree
from Cornell University and pursued a career as
a civil engineer. On April 5, 1925, he responded to
an advertisement offering a flying boat for sale in
Portland, Oregon, where he lived at the time. This
started his career as a bush pilot, and on May 26,
1925 he arrived at Ketchikan, Alaska. Merrill was the
first to fly to many cities in Alaska; the first airport
in Anchorage was named Merrill Field in his honor.
On September 16, 1929, Merrill departed on a flight
from Anchorage to the Nyac mine near Bethel,
Alaska, and was never seen again.

Joe Crosson's Winter Parka
Joe Crosson arrived in Alaska in 1926 to fly for the
Fairbanks Airplane Company. Within the year, he
was a famous international aviation celebrity and
a recognized authority on flying and survival in the
harsh Alaskan environment. Crosson's exceptional
career went beyond his polar and glacier flying. He
was well known for mercy missions, which included
his delivery of diphtheria serum to the North Coast
in 1931 and assisting Wiley Post resume his world
flights in 1931 and 1933. Crosson wore this cotton
duck, sheepskin, and leather-trimmed parka during
his flying career in Alaska.

BUSH-PILOT TOOL KIT

BUSH-PILOT TOOL KIT

I would get that airplane warmed up and ready for departure. We drained the oil at night and then brought it into the office where it wouldn't congeal. It wasn't real warm there, but it was a lot warmer than outside. In the morning we would warm it up with the plumber's pot to get it good and hot.

You've got the engine cover on, and you'd start heating the airplane up with two fire pots. When the airplane got warm enough, you would take one of the fire pots out and set the oil on that fire pot to get it boiling hot to dump it in. The fire pots were just the same fire pots that the plumbers used in the early days to melt the lead hot, red hot, to seal up the cast-iron joints when you were doing plumbing work. The oil had its own container, a can specially built where you could set it right on top of your plumber's pot to get it good and hot. [...] You got those fire pots going underneath the airplane in an open fifty-gallon drum with air spaces in between so it would get plenty of air to torch.

But you had to stay by them if you were running two fire pots because if one went out, then you'd have to get in there real quick and drag it out of there because it will shoot raw gas up and catch your airplane on fire.[41]

Holger "Jorgy" Jorgensen

Flying in Alaska was as much about the ground as the air. Take-offs from snow and landings on gravel bars or glaciers were as hazardous as the mountain updrafts and downdrafts. When the bush pilot set down for the night, the work was not over. Airplanes required maintenance. A pilot's dual role was as a mechanic. On a winter morning an airplane could not take off in the frigid temperatures; engines needed to be warmed, which was a well rehearsed ritual of the northern bush pilot. Another chore of winter flying was the removal of snow and ice from the wings and skis. Bob Reeve had to blowtorch the ice from underneath his glacier skis to be able to take off. Frost was also a constant enemy. Only a fraction of an inch of new frost, which could accumulate within a few minutes' unloading time on the ground, was sufficient to destroy the lift of an airplane's airfoil. "The last thing you did before take-off," said Reeve, "was to take a rope and slide it back and forth along the wing and remove the last coating of frost."[42] The empennage, the horizontal and vertical stabilizers, had to be cleared as well.

Emergency landings necessitated another array of skills and equipment. Crashing in Alaska posed the risks of hypothermia, wild animals, and insurmountable distances from aid. Each bush pilot therefore had his or her own version of an emergency survival kit. Noel Wien carried a spare wooden propeller, small compass, mosquito net, and Luger pistol. Secured in his cockpit were pliers, a wrench, screwdriver, and a Boy Scout knife.[43] Inside his airplane, even for short flights, Bob Reeve carried a fire pot, extinguisher, motor and wing covers, sleeping bag, emergency food, rifle, axe, shovel, magazines, and a deck of cards.[44]

Fuel was another issue. Due to the remoteness of Alaska and its villages, pilots had to plan ahead. They had to have oil and gas ready at the next stop; otherwise, they would not make it back. There were no airports for fuel and gas, so supplies were staged. Oil and gas cans were stationed around air routes, villages, and roadhouses.

A bush pilot had to have an airplane capable of operating in many different environments – air, land, water, and ice. Most of the early airplanes in Alaska were surplus. The standard equipment involved an inaccurate altimeter, an oil-pressure gauge, and a water-temperature gauge. Most Alaskan planes also had to be adapted to accommodate skis and floats. Parts were not easy to come by, so often skis and

Bob Reeve works on his airplane with Owen Meals and others in service of the Ruff & Tuff Mine near Valdez, 1937.

Keeping the engine warm on a Pilgrim in the cold winter.

floats were handmade. Many aircraft also relied on tough, oversized tires called "tundra tires" to handle the problems of landing on rocky stream banks or spongy turf. Adaptations of standard parts were necessary to make Arctic flying possible.

Bob Reeve was well known for modifying his airplane for better performance, much to the chagrin of safety inspectors who were not always fans of his ingenuity and inventiveness. To suit his work servicing the mines in the mountains around Valdez, Reeve moved his aircraft's ski pedestal rearward so that he could better climb out of water. He also extended his tail wings, and attached a home-built supercharger that gave his engines close to sea-level performance at high altitudes.

Similarly, Noel Wien developed new flying methods with his retrofitted airplane for take-offs from tight Alaskan landing zones. His Standard lifted off in a nose-level attitude and then needed to be held down to allow his air speed to build, but mountainous terrain prevented a continued nose-down flight. So Wien would alternate between pressure and release on short take-offs to get the ultimate climb from his aircraft. For landing on short fields and sandbars, Wien learned to cut power only at the absolutely necessary moment, and only for the absolutely necessary duration. He and other pilots were adept at knowing the limits of the airplanes and how much they could test them.

Aviation in the Territory of Alaska was individualized and competitive, with rates that often varied wildly. There also was no real supervision of operations or maintenance, no general safety rules. Pilots landed anywhere, however and wherever they felt they could set a plane down and survive. Freight loads were the bush pilot's bread and butter. "Our loads were determined by the length of the field and

Joe Crosson with the airplane wreckage of Carl Ben Eielson's Hamilton Metalplane in the Siberian Arctic. Crosson, accompanied by Harold Gillam, was searching for the missing pilot, mechanic, Earl Borland, and the airplane and landed at the site located approximately six miles from a cabin used by a witness who had reported hearing Eielson's airplane overhead in November 1929.

whether we could make it off the ground," said pilot Ray Petersen. "We'd fill up all the seats, throw in all the freight our passengers' laps would hold, fill up the gas tanks, and take off. On a long trip we could take an extra load, because as the gas burned out we got the additional lift we needed to make it over the pass."[45]

Overloaded airplanes were a danger and likely the biggest cause of accidents next to, or in combination with, dangerous flying weather. No one but the bush pilot controlled how much freight was loaded. There were some cursory inspections, but bush pilots paid little heed. "When Brewster [the inspector] was around," said Petersen, "we'd all wait till he went to lunch, then everybody would overload their planes and take off fast. One of the biggest reasons for 'crack-ups' was 'that last ten bucks' worth of freight."[46]

While goods posed one problem, services posed another. Flying passengers was a significant responsibility. Passengers were entirely dependent upon a pilot for their safety, and in a forced landing it was the bush pilot's responsibility to keep them alive. Sam White recalled: "It can be a tremendous job to protect passengers who are inadequately dressed. They will travel in winter in Oxford shoes, cotton socks, and business suits, dresses and high-heeled slippers. It seems they place a higher premium on appearances than they do on life and comfort, and they seem not to mind giving their pilot plenty to worry about."[47]

Unloading freight was not always straightforward, either. Bob Reeve learned to drop his loads without stopping his airplane in order to deliver goods to mountainside mining camps. Bill Egan, who later became the first governor of Alaska, worked for Reeve to make airdrops of supplies. They would load the airplane, then take off with the cargo door removed and a rope around Egan so that he would not slip out with the freight.

The airplanes used in Alaska beginning in the 1920s reflected technological development that was gaining momentum overall in the United States and Europe. The first aircraft to have a sustained presence, the Curtiss JN "Jenny," Standard J-1, and the de Havilland DH-4B, were World War I-surplus biplanes. They featured open cockpits, wood structures and fabric-coverings held together by strut-and-wire bracing, water-cooled inline engines, and wood propellers. Each of these fragile aircraft was susceptible to easy damage in the harsh and unforgiving Alaskan environment. Wood structural components and propellers deteriorated rapidly, radiators and cooling systems froze solid if not drained between flights, and the elements overall eliminated an airplane's ability to take to the sky very quickly.

Improvements in aeronautical technology increased performance. New aircraft with high-wing monoplane wings and sturdy tubular steel fuselages and landing gear appeared. Manufacturers such as Bellanca, Fairchild, Stearman, and Travel Air soon became brands that generated their own loyal followings in Alaska aviation.

In terms of propulsion, the air-cooled radial engine, a power plant with the cylinders arranged around the crankcase like the petals on a flower, and the metal propeller were cornerstones in aviation. Radials from the Wright Aeronautical Corporation and Pratt & Whitney Aircraft provided more power, up to 350 horsepower in a light, reliable, and compact shape. New propellers with aluminum alloy blades and steel hubs from Hamilton Standard enabled safer flying from cramped and remote flying strips and lakes. These technologies, which became

An Alaska Coastal Airlines Bellanca airplane is pulled up to the beach in Southcentral Alaska. Alaska Coastal Airlines was an airline formed in Juneau in 1939 as a result of a merger of Alaska Air Transport and Marine Airways. On April 1, 1962, Alaska Coastal Airlines merged with Ellis Air Lines, trading for a while as Alaska Coastal-Ellis Airlines. Alaska Coastal Airlines was taken over by Alaska Airlines in April 1968. Although the cargo has changed from goods and services for the local community to that of a tourist economy, Juneau's waterfront remains a major seaport for ships and floatplanes.

standard equipment on the bush planes of the 1930s and 1940s, enhanced survivability in the harsh year-round environment of Alaska.

The terrain of Alaska also shaped the technology found in bush planes, especially in terms of the undercarriage, or landing gear. Depending on the season, the part of Alaska from which they were operating, and the particular mission, a bush pilot operated from water, land, or snow.

The predominance of tens of thousands of lakes all over the region facilitated the use of a pair of floats, the long slender boat-like hulls that allowed aircraft to operate off the water. The first floats were wood and deteriorated rapidly. The introduction of the aluminum float by the Edo Aircraft Corporation in the 1920s ensured that seaplanes were strong enough to operate in the harsh Alaska environment. Edo and other manufacturers quickly offered floats for a variety of different aircraft. Today, the Lake Hood Seaplane Base in Anchorage is home to approximately 800 float and seaplanes and is the world's busiest with an average of 190 flights a day.

Regular-sized tires, as found on an airplane fresh from a factory, proved to be unable to withstand repeated landings on rough airfields, improvised landing sites, beaches, tidal flats, and sand and gravel bars in rivers. To improve landing and taxiing performance, Bob Reeve improvised his own "tundra tires" – balloon-shaped tires with smooth treads that made landing on rough terrain easier. Recognizing the need, the Goodyear Tire and Rubber Company and others offered balloon tires in diameters upwards of thirty inches. The Alaskan Bushwheel Company fills that need today and tundra tires have become a popular accessory for pilots in and out of Alaska.[48]

Early on, it was clear that winter flying meant that rubber tires, oversized or not, were not practical. Carl Ben Eielson, Noel Wien, Bob Reeve, and the other pioneering bush pilots installed homemade wood skis in the place of wheels on their aircraft to extend their capabilities in winter. As air services grew, operators made their own skis for a variety of aircraft. Some of the largest were for the Ford Tri-Motor airliner. The early improvised skis consisted of wood runners with steel frames and bands for reinforcement. Specialty businesses such as the Federal Ski Company produced dedicated skis made from aluminum and steel. Beginning in the 1950s, Airglas, Inc., produced lightweight fiberglass skis.

The installation of aircraft skis could be a tedious exercise, which involved lifting the entire airplane and removing of the wheels. For long winters, dedicated ski use was acceptable providing the bush pilot stayed in tune with when the conversion back to wheels needed to take place. One problem the bush pilots often encountered was terrain suitable for both skis and wheels in a single day, particularly when glacier flying or operating from tidal flats during the spring and summer. The solution was the addition of a retractable ski to wheeled landing gear. The pilot pumped a lever in the cockpit that lowered the skis for snow landings and raised them for conventional landings. De Havilland in Canada pioneered the development of hydraulic wheel-skis in the 1950s.

After World War II, working pilots in Alaska embraced the new general aviation aircraft that emerged in the late 1940s. The de Havilland Beaver, one of the ever-present bush planes, appeared with a 400-horsepower Pratt & Whitney R-985 radial engine. Aircraft from Cessna and Piper featured all-metal construction, ready adaptation to floats, tundra tires, or skis, and new air-cooled opposed engines. The arrangement of the cylinders horizontally across from each other led them to be called opposed engines. Continental and Lycoming produced them in four- and six-cylinder configurations in the 150- to 250-horsepower range. For bush pilots seeking performance above all else, the new engines were small, light in weight, cheap, and powerful. The Helio Courier offered short-take-off-and-landing performance at a level unmatched any other aircraft, but was produced in smaller numbers. Considered today to be classics, bush planes such as the Beaver, Courier, Cessna 185, and Piper Super Cub made flying practical and affordable in Alaska.

There was a cultural symbolism embedded in bush plane landing gear technology after World War II. The generations of bush pilots that followed the early pioneers made a living in Alaska with these innovations. Today, the use of that technology reinforces the romantic image of the bush pilot for recreational fliers and hunting guides and charter operators bringing outsiders to Alaska. In other words, the choice of landing gear is all about image. An experienced bush pilot, F.E. Potts, remarked:

There is no question that the type of life one could lead in the Alaska of the 1960s, in its freedom, self-reliance and overall quality, is a compelling image for many people today. Huge tires, along with skis and floats, are unquestionably part of that image.[49]

Today's bush planes require fewer adaptations to make them ready to fly in the Arctic. The classic Beavers, Super Cubs, and Cessna 185s still dominate bush flying because of their rugged construction and availability of parts. Of course, the costs of modern airplanes and aviation gas are prohibitive. The new survival kit for the bush pilot is cash, a smartphone, and GPS. GPS data and smart phones with real-time weather reports are available with a click.

The Alaskan Airways Fairchild 71 flown by Joe Crosson in the early 1930s was especially suited to flying around Mt. McKinley. The 450-horsepower radial engine and metal propeller gave it the necessary power to carry tourists sightseeing, determine the true height of the mountain, or deliver climbers and their gear to base camp. The tubular steel fuselage and purpose-built skis were rugged enough for rough glacier landings. The 71 had folding wings, which Crosson used to save the airplane when he was forced to stay overnight in a storm on Muldrow Glacier.

Native Winter Parka
The height of bush pilot style of the late 1940s and 1950s was the Native-style fur parka. Fairbanks physician Paul B. Haggland wore this parka, made from muskrat pelts, wolf's hair, and bead ornamentation, on his medical rounds. His bush pilot son, Pete, went on to have a successful fifty-year career in Alaska aviation.

Petroleum Products Used in Alaska
Aviation gasoline and oil were precious commodities for bush pilots. They often staged cans along their routes to keep their aircraft operating. Other products like Ban-Ice, which prevented moisture in fuel systems from freezing, and Blazo Fuel for portable heaters and stoves, increased the chances of survival. Creative bush pilots, as well as villagers, found innovative ways to use the empty cans and crates. Improvised furniture made from crates came to be known as "Alaskan Chippendale." The detritus of bush flying became part of everyday life in Alaska.

Aircraft Skis

The installation of skis on aircraft enabled take-offs and landings from snow, ice, and mud making flying a year-round activity in Alaska.

These Federal skis (top) from the late 1940s were an answer to the difficulty of removing wheels and installing skis on a seasonal basis. Operators simply clamped and secured these to the wheeled landing gear of an airplane and removed them when no longer needed.

United Airmotive manufactured these Model 25B skis (left), intended for small aircraft like the Piper Super Cub, at Merrill Field in Anchorage in August 1952.

Based in Minneapolis, Minnesota, the Federal Aircraft Works produced the "The Federal Ski" (right). The SA4 wood ski appeared in the late 1930s for use on light aircraft.

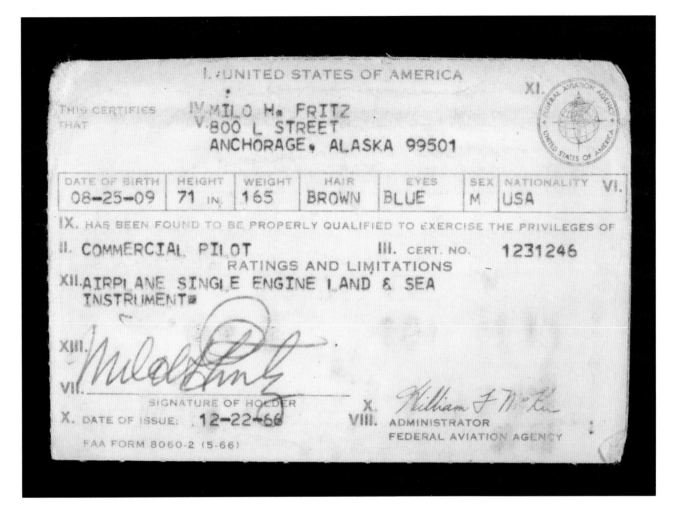

Milo Fritz Pilot's License and log books,
issued by the Federal Aviation Administration
in 1966.
An aviation and medicine pioneer in Alaska, Dr. Milo
Fritz was an eye, ear, nose, and throat surgeon who
came to Alaska in the 1940s with his wife, Betsy,
a nurse. He began a practice that took him into
almost every remote community of the Territory
of Alaska, to areas where there were no doctors,
no clinics, no health care facilities of any kind. The
area he served covered almost a quarter of Alaska's
586,000 square miles, from Anchorage northeast
to the Canadian border near Fort Yukon, west to
Bettles and Huslia, south to Anvik and Shageluk,
and east again over the Chugach Mountains to
Anchorage. Dozens of villages in that vast expanse
would never have seen a doctor if Fritz had not
traveled by dog sled or small boat, or piloted his
own single-engine airplane. A command surgeon
for the 11th Air force in World War II, Milo spent
much of his service time in Alaska.

Goodyear Air Wheel
The Goodyear Tire and Rubber Company pioneered the development of aircraft tires. In the late 1920s, the company introduced a new balloon tire invented by A. J. Musselman. The tire connected directly to the hub in place of the wheel. The combination of low pressure with high volume air acted as a shock absorber on rough terrain, a quality much desired by the bush pilots of Alaska.

Herman Nelson Portable Aircraft Heater
Dealing with the extreme temperatures in the Arctic was a constant challenge and a labor intensive activity. Pilots could not simply shut down their engine, park their airplane, and leave it unattended overnight in subzero temperatures. Portable heaters such as this Herman Nelson BT400 from the mid-1950s ensured that engine oil did not turn into jelly and crankcases did not go through the physical shock of cold inactivity to hot operation, which would lead to their destruction. They also proved vital to heating aircraft cabins.

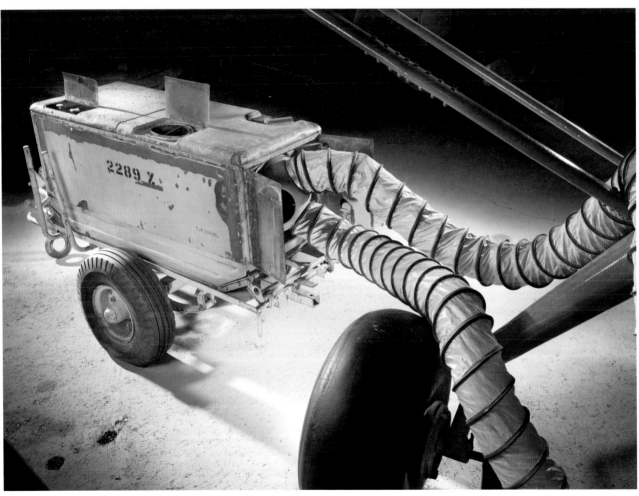

Arctic Cat Model 560-D Snow Machine
By the 1960s, the snow machine, better known as the snowmobile outside the region, displaced traditional animal-powered means of ground transportation in rural Alaska. As a bush pilot arrived with mail, goods, and passengers, a common sight was villagers on snow machines swarming the bush plane. Some simply wanted to see what the bush plane had brought. Others unloaded the cargo onto a sleigh pulled by heavy-duty machines like this Arctic Cat 560-D for distribution to the community. The arrival of supplies by air was a vital lifeline that ensured the village's survival in a harsh arctic environment. Snow machines also carried villagers and goods to the bush plane, which served as the first step toward the outside world.

**ALASKAN AVIATION
ON THE FRONT LINES**

ALASKAN AVIATION ON THE FRONT LINES

In February 1935, in a speech before the House Military Affairs Committee, outspoken prophet of military aviation and former general William "Billy" Mitchell declared, "Alaska is the most central place in the world for aircraft [...]. I believe in the future he who holds Alaska will hold the world, and I think it is the most strategic place in the world." Mitchell recommended that Army Air Corps units be positioned at strategic points throughout the Territory and on the Aleutian chain. The islands' strategic value was their control of Pacific Great Circle Routes. The Japanese reasoned that control of the Aleutians would prevent a possible U.S. attack across the Northern Pacific. Similarly, the U.S. feared that the islands would be used as bases from which to launch aerial assaults against the West Coast.

Thus, as Mitchell predicted, in World War II the Aleutian Islands were host to battle. Starting on June 3, 1942, the Japanese initiated the Aleutians campaign when a small force occupied the islands of Attu and Kiska while carrier units attacked Dutch Harbor. The move was part of a dual campaign waged in conjunction with the Battle of Midway and was the only Japanese incursion into the Western Hemisphere on American soil. There were three combatants during the campaign, the Allies consisting of American and Canadian forces, the Japanese Army and Navy, and the terrain and weather of the Aleutians.

Attu and Kiska were on the westernmost edge of the Aleutians. American military and naval forces conducted primarily an aerial bombardment siege, which was a significant challenge. Kiska was a Japanese stronghold with a submarine base, seaplane hangars, military barracks, and naval and supply ships in the harbor with plenty of anti-aircraft batteries for protection. The main American airfields at Umnak meant it would be a 1,200-mile round trip to Kiska for 11th Air Force bombers, a long distance that was deadly and detrimental to successful operations due to the weather. The creation of a second airfield at Adak shortened the distance by 700 miles in September 1942. Within days, units under the command of Col. William O. Eareckson launched the first combined low-level zero-altitude attack with bombers and fighters. The shorter distance allowed a shift in focus to attacking Kiska rather than fighting the weather. John Huston's wartime film, *Report from the Aleutians* (1943), captured operations from Adak for American theater-goers. A new airfield at Amchitka established in January 1943 put American bombers and fighters only fifty miles away from Kiska.

The Allied goal during the Aleutians campaign was to eject the Japanese forces from American soil. The bloody Battle of Attu in May 1943 was one of the costliest invasions for the United States in the Pacific. The poor weather limited the use of airpower, which led to innovations in air-ground communications to enhance the tactical use of aircraft. Once taken, Attu served as the base for American army and navy bombers as they attacked Japanese territory.

Weather made the Aleutians the world's toughest air theater.[50] Williwaws blew in all directions wreaking havoc on airfield operations and damaged aircraft and the makeshift living structures on the ground. In flight, the sudden blast of air could push an aircraft thousands of feet in any direction, jarring its crew and potentially wrecking it in the process. Unfavorable headwinds could extend a four-hour mission to ten. Constant turbulence was in the air. Traditionally, pilots trained to avoid bad weather by flying higher. In the Aleutians, that resulted in fatal aircraft icing. They had to fly lower, which increased the possibility of hitting a mountain or a ship on

Photograph of a burning Japanese ship in Kiska Harbor after U.S. Army Air Forces units raided Japanese-held Kiska Island. This photograph was made from a Navy plane shortly after the bombing.

the water. Navigation was problematic due to the lack of accurate charts and zero-visibility. Frenetic electrical activity interfered with radio navigation aids. In terms of morale, the feeling of isolation for personnel and the constantly wet, muddy, and cold living conditions was excruciating. The bitter cold and corrosion-inducing environment made mechanical systems such as bomb releases and machine guns faulty, froze engines solid, and covered aircraft in sheets of ice. The Army Air Force's Cold Weather Test Laboratory at Fairbanks, worked to determine methods of safe operation and survival in arctic weather. They freely adopted bush pilot techniques to survive in the Aleutians and Alaska.

There were significant losses of aircrew and aircraft without enemy engagement. During fall of 1942, the 11th Air Force lost nine aircraft in combat while losing sixty-three to weather and mechanical trouble. Overall, Allied forces lost fifty-six aircraft in combat out of 471 lost overall. The remainder of that number was caused by weather and mechanical problems. The Japanese lost sixty-nine aircraft in combat and approximately 200 to fog and storms.

The air, land, and sea campaign to retake the Aleutians concluded with the bloodless invasion of Kiska in August 1943. It was the first theater-wide victory in World War II for the United States and

As part of the Lend-Lease Program, the Russians set up command centers in Fairbanks and Nome where their pilots were trained to take over the aircraft and fly them to Siberia and on to various fronts in western Russia. The first group of Russian pilots arrived at Nome on August 14, 1942, on their way to Ladd Field in Fairbanks. The first Lend-Lease aircraft, a group of 12 A-20 Havocs, arrived at Ladd Field on September 3, 1942. The first Russian pilots, after five days of training on the aircraft, took off for Nome and the long trip to the Eastern Front. The aircraft were supplied with Russian language operations and maintenance manuals, as well as painted in Red Air Force camouflage colors and national markings. Above, the national insignia, a red star with a white border, is painted on a plane at Great Falls, Montana.

This Bell fighter crash-landed at Nome on the way to the Soviet Union.

foreshadowed an increased military and federal presence in Alaska. Known today as the "Forgotten War," the Aleutians campaign was overshadowed by the simultaneous Guadalcanal operation in the Solomon Islands in the South Pacific.

When the war broke out, bush pilots offered their services for the defense of Alaska, but they were told that they were not wanted in the Army. What they were doing, however, was exactly what was needed. Between the Morrison-Knudsen Construction Company and the Army Corps of Engineers, all sorts of projects were underway at the same time, and Morrison-Knudsen was hiring all the experienced bush pilots they could get. In 1942, Mudhole Smith quit Cordova Air

Service and went to work for Morrison-Knudsen, as did Harold Gillam, who founded Gillam Airways in 1932. Gillam became chief pilot for the Morrison-Knudsen. Bob Reeve, too, moved his operations to the Aleutians, seeing the opportunity for work and profit.

The Alaska Territorial Guard (ATG) or "Eskimo Scouts" was a reserve force component of the U.S. Army organized in 1942. The ATG was made up of volunteers, most of whom were too old or too young to be drafted, from approximately 100 Native communities throughout Alaska. The ATG performed many vital services for the Allied effort until 1947 when its operation ceased, including safeguarding a source of platinum against Japanese attack, securing the terrain near the

Col. Russell Keillor (left), the commanding officer of Ladd Field, Brig. Gen. Dale V. Gaffney (center), commander of the Alaskan Division, Air Transport Command, and Col. Peter S. Kisilev (right) recognize the delivery of 5,000th aircraft to the Soviet Air Force on September 10, 1944. Aircraft like the Bell P-63 Kingcobra fighter shown here proved important in Soviet operations against both Nazi Germany and Imperial Japan late in World War II.

vital air route between the United States and Russia, and maintaining survival caches along transportation corridors and coastal regions. In addition to their official duties, ATG members were noted for successfully promoting racial integration within the U.S. military. In 2000, all ATG members were granted U.S. veteran status. Some of the members are still living, including noted pilot Jorgy Jorgensen.

Most American soldiers were not prepared to fight in northern climates. As the Department of Defense sought information about flying and fighting in such an environment, it consulted Joe Crosson. When Crosson was General Manager of Pacific Alaska Airways (PAA) in the late 1930s, the company provided the U.S. military with hard-earned knowledge gathered by pilots and mechanics during their decades of work in the Arctic. PAA's experience in developing wing covers, skis, engine preheating, radio communications, and navigation aids gave the military valuable insight into flying in the North. PAA also let the military use its facilities in Alaska. When the Army Air Corps hired polar explorer Vilhajalmur Stefansson to write an Arctic survival manual, Stefansson looked to Crosson for information based on his survival experiences.

In 1943, chief of the Army Air Forces, General Henry H. "Hap" Arnold, recommended Crosson for temporary full-time service with a group of civilians who were charged with analyzing military operations in the Aleutian Islands. The group toured the Aleutian theater of operations. The Army's official history of the group singled out Crosson and weather forecaster Howard J. Thompson of Anchorage: "In short order, Crosson and Thompson made surveys of conditions in their specialized fields, pointing out deficiencies in the military set-up and suggesting in detail improved procedures in light of civilian

experience with local conditions. By the time these men left in July 1943, programs for improving operations along the lines they had recommended were already underway."[51]

In December 1942, a geodetic control unit arrived in Fairbanks from the First Mapping Group, Bolling Field, Washington, D.C. Their assignment was to obtain astronomical observations to establish the precise latitude and longitude of designated ground control points in the interior of Alaska. These points were prominent natural features and small settlements. The points were to be used with charts of aerial photography, which the Army Air Forces had taken from an altitude of 20,000 feet in the summer of 1941. The aerial photos were so secret that they were not given names, only numbers. The Army Air Forces refused to allow the numbers correlated with locations to leave Washington, D.C. The only way one could determine the location of a photo was to have seen and recognized the area. Bush pilot Sam White memorized much of the area that was involved:

Early on, I had many arguments with the crew about where the photos were taken. I looked at a picture and told them that lake, or that bend in the river, or that island, is at such and such a place. For some time they wouldn't buy it. After many trips to the wrong areas they let me decide where the photos were taken and allowed me to fly them there to establish an exact control location.[52]

White also noted that when Army crews arrived in Alaska, they assumed that there were towns and hotels everywhere. On maps they had seen place names and presumed that each was a town with a hotel. However, many named places on Alaskan maps were nothing but abandoned mines or even trappers' cabins.

After World War II, the U.S. Air Force initiated "ptarmigan" missions from Fairbanks, Alaska to the North Pole. Named after the Arctic bird native to the Territory, the flights recorded weather data on a continual basis by the Air Force and weather bureaus across North America. The crew of the Boeing B-29 Polar Queen from the 375th Weather Reconnaissance Squadron flew the 100th ptarmigan mission in August 1948.

GREATEST AIR SPECTACLE OF THE JET AGE!

FU-190

Earth-shaking, sky-shattering . . . SO BIG it took years to make!

HOWARD HUGHES'
JET PILOT
Starring
JOHN WAYNE · JANET LEIGH
AND THE
U. S. AIR FORCE
TECHNICOLOR®

WITH JAY C. FLIPPEN   PAUL FIX   HANS CONRIED   Directed by JOSEF von STERNBERG · Written and Produced by JULES FURTHMAN

Jet Pilot is a 1957 Cold War action film starring John Wayne and Janet Leigh. The 94th FS and its parent 1st Fighter Group had just finished a deployment to Ladd Air Force Base in Fairbanks, Alaska, as depicted in the storyline.

While military aviation became embedded in the Territory, Alaska also served as an important aerial byway during World War II. After the June 1941 Nazi Invasion of the Soviet Union and the Japanese attack on Pearl Harbor later in December, the United States extended its Lend-Lease war material program to its communist ally. The Soviets needed aircraft to wage war against the Nazis on the Eastern Front. Established in September 1942, a new 2,450-mile military airway called the ALSIB (short for Alaska-Siberia) served as a direct connection between U.S. aircraft factories and the Soviet Air Force. Beginning in Great Falls, Montana, the pilots of the Army Air Force's Air Transport Command ferried military bombers and fighters across Canada to Ladd Field near Fairbanks for inspection by Soviet officials. Once accepted, Soviet pilots ferried the aircraft west to Krasnoyarsk in Siberia by way of Nome. The ALSIB saw 7,926 military aircraft, primarily Bell P-39 Airacobra and P-63 Kingcobra fighters, Douglas A-20 Havoc and North American B-25 Mitchell bombers, and Douglas C-47 Skytrain transports, pass through Ladd Field.

The ALSIB pilots and other personnel faced the well-known challenges of flying in Alaska. The demands of supplying the Soviets meant they had to fly in unpredictable weather, zero visibility, and rough and remote terrain regardless of the season. The bitterly cold winter of 1942–1943 pushed the development of arctic flying and survival gear and search-and-rescue procedures. Ground crews adopted bush pilot practice, such as the use of canvas covers over the wings and tails of aircraft to protect their aerodynamic integrity while heaters prevented the valuable engines from freezing. Pilots resorted to flying along the strategically important Alaskan Highway, which paralleled the series of airfields on the route. They used the

View of Sigurd Wien landing the Noorduyn Norseman airplane loaded with DEW (Distance Early Warning) Line radar equipment at Cross Island, Alaska, east of Barrow, 1947. Photograph by Noel Wien.

highway as a landing field in times of emergency. By the time the ferry program ended in September 1945, a total of 133 aircraft were lost due to weather or pilot error.

No country benefited more from a war than Alaska. As a result of its important role in World War II, Alaska received fifty airports and thousands of miles of navigational airways. By the time of the Pearl Harbor attack in 1941, the Civil Aeronautics Administration (CAA) had constructed 4,000 miles of operating airways in the name of national defense. Within three years, there were over 7,000, and by 1946 some 8,300.[53] The CAA created an all-weather airways system using the latest technology that directly benefitted military transportation and commercial aviation. Having developed aviation on its own, with no federal aid, and having operated without communications or paved runways until the war, Alaska found itself by 1945 equipped with a network of airways as good as, and often better than, those anywhere else in the U.S. A near-endless supply

of military surplus multi-engine transports flooded the market and an enterprising bush pilot could purchase and build his own little Alaskan aviation empire.

As the world transitioned from World War II to the Cold War, with the United States and the Soviet Union standing on the precipice of nuclear war, Alaska continued to be a critical strategic area. In terms of location, the territory was the closest American possession to the Soviet Union, which placed it on the front line. From Alaska, the American military monitored the activities of the Soviets and stood at the ready to resist an Arctic invasion. Moreover, the region offered the military vast areas to train, operate, and develop new methods of Arctic warfare. Regarding industry, Alaska possessed natural resources crucial to the emerging military-industrial complex of the 1950s. The unprecedented investment in terms of infrastructure and resources in Alaska increased exponentially beginning in the 1950s, which resulted in what one historian termed a "militarized

Two U.S. Air Force General Dynamics F-16 Fighting Falcon fighters from the 343rd Wing, Pacific Air Forces, assigned to Eielson Air Force Base, Fairbanks, in 1991. The 343rd traced its history back to the first fighter units to arrive in Alaska in the early days of World War II in 1942.

landscape."[54] The destinies of the American military, federal government, and Alaska became intimately linked.

The shortest distance between the United States and the Soviet Union was a route through the Arctic. With the establishment of the U.S. Air Force in 1947, fighter interceptor and long-range atomic bomber units based at Eielson and Elmendorf air force bases, in Fairbanks and Anchorage respectively, were on constant alert. They were on the front line of American defense, strategically poised to blunt a Soviet attack or spearhead an American blow against the enemy. A system of radar stations stretching from the Aleutians to the North Coast of Alaska and on through Canada, Greenland, and Iceland provided advanced detection of any Soviet airborne threats. Building the Distant-Early Warning Line (DEW, or "Dew" Line as it was called) from 1954 to 1957 required one of the largest airlifts in history. The bush pilots of Alaska, well-versed in Arctic flying, became crucial to the operation as work crews labored through the sunless winter to complete the DEW line. When advances in ballistic missile technology made the continental lower forty-eight states an easier target from the Soviet Union, the Ballistic Missile Early Warning System, which includes a station at Clear Air Force Station in central Alaska, began operations in 1959. All air-defense operations in Alaska came under the umbrella of the North American Air Defense Command, a joint operation between the United States and Canada, beginning in 1961.

The presence of the U.S. Air Force, Army, and Navy brought tremendous social, economic, and political changes to Alaska during the Cold War. In the wake of the dissolution of the Soviet Union in 1991, the federal government, specifically the Department of Defense and its various services, continues to be the state's number one employer.

Military flight helmet with goggles
Worn by Captain James A. Diefenbeck of the U.S. Army Air Forces, who flew combat missions in the Aleutians and Europe during WWII. Both American and Japanese pilots found the severe weather in the Aleutians to be as dangerous as their enemies.

Alaska Territorial Guard (ATG) medal and patch.
This medal was presented to Tommy M. Ongtooguk, who enlisted in the Alaska Territorial Guard at Nome. He was issued a National Guard Enfield rifle and an ATG patch, which was sewn onto a white hunting parka. Ongtooguk later entered the Army and Army Air Forces. The patch was worn on the shoulder and the stars form the big dipper, now seen on Alaska's state flag.

Military rank patches, Alaska Air Command.
This collection of military rank patches reflects William J. Niemi's service with the 297th infantry of the Alaska National Guard and the U.S. Corps of Engineers during WWII. He then worked for the Alaska Road Commission and later the Federal Highway Administration out of Juneau, Alaska. He is recognized for many roads, brides, and landing strips built under his administration.

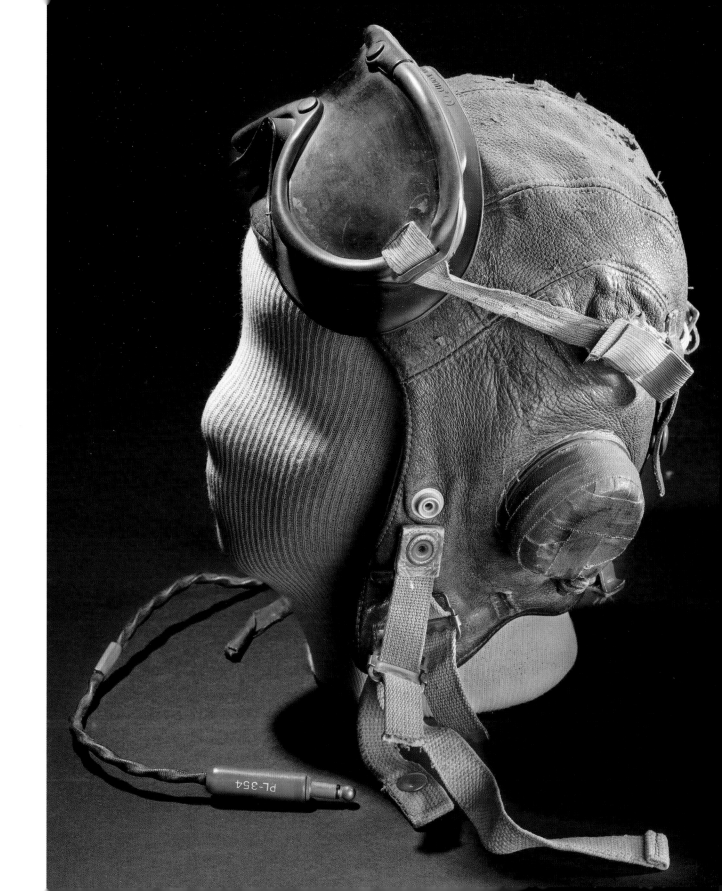

World War II Mission Board, Adak Museum, Aleutian Islands.
This chalkboard from 1943 hung in the Adak Museum in the Aleutian Islands. The board recreated the history of American flight casualties in Alaska during WWII. The U.S. military constructed bases in the western Aleutian Islands from which to launch operations against the Japanese. Adak Island was chosen as the site of an airfield, and flight operations began in September 1942.

Military Flight Jacket
Sheep shearling-lined leather flying jacket.

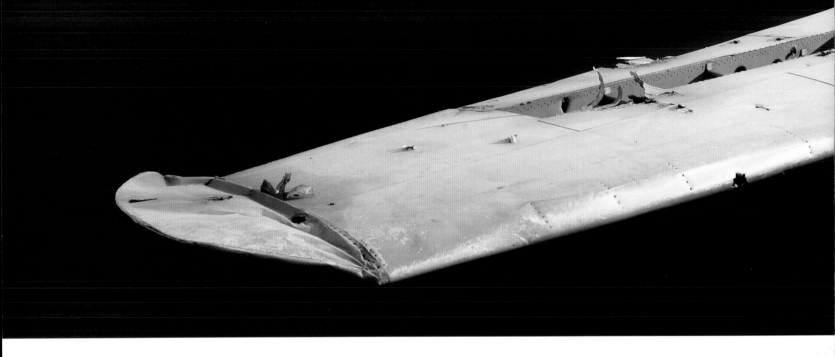

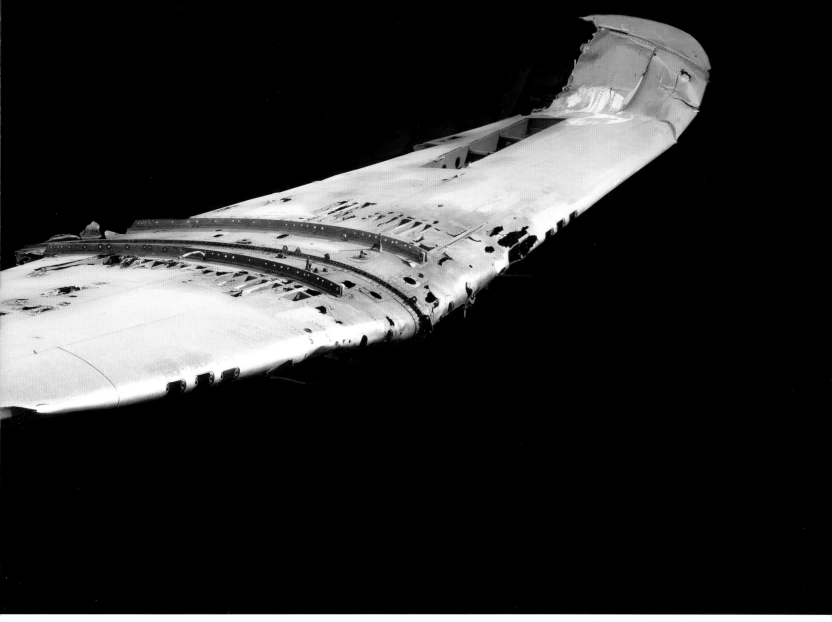

Curtiss P-40E Warhawk Wing
Imperial Japanese Navy bombers and fighters successfully attacked American installations on the second day of the Battle of Dutch Harbor in the Aleutians on June 4, 1942. As eight of them regrouped over Unalaska Island to return to their aircraft carrier, they encountered an equal number of Curtiss P-40 Warhawk fighters from the 11th Fighter Squadron. During the ensuing dogfight, a Japanese Zero fighter attacked Lt. W. Edward McIntyre, Jr. and his Warhawk caught fire. McIntyre crash landed and survived to receive the Purple Heart for the injuries sustained during his first combat mission. This is the wing from McIntyre's P-40.

Diary of a Soviet pilot in Alaska, 1942-1945
With the initiation of the ALSIB airway, a new generation of Russians in Soviet uniforms arrived in Alaska to accept and continue the delivery of American military aircraft. After overcoming initial difficulties with the language barrier and military customs, the Soviets enjoyed Fairbanks and Nome and the camaraderie with their American contemporaries. The harmonious relationship was a victim of the war's conclusion and the ever-deepening cultural freeze of the Cold War. This hand-written diary from Victor Dmitrievich Glazkov, a navigator and radioman, recounts his days in Alaska and Siberia flying the aerial bridge between North America and Asia.

Marsden Matting
Just before World War II, the U.S. Army developed Marsden matting for the rapid construction of temporary aircraft runways, landing strips, and taxi ways anywhere they may be needed. The perforated steel sheet was strong, rigid, and facilitated the draining of water. The interlocking sides created a solid and level surface. The use of Marsden matting was prolific in all combat theaters, but was used on a large scale in Alaska, especially in the remote Aleutians. The airfield at Umnak featured 3 million square feet of Marsden matting on a 3,000 by 100 foot runway in 1942.

Bell P-39 Airacobra Wing
The United States supplied warplanes to the Soviet Union through the Lend Lease program from September 1942 to September 1945. As factory-fresh fighters, bombers, and transports arrived at Great Falls, Montana, on their way to delivery in Fairbanks, workers painted over the blue and white U.S. national insignia on the wings and fuselages of the aircraft with the red star of the Soviet Union. This is a wing from a P-39 fighter that collided with another aircraft and crashed sixty miles east of Fairbanks. Traces of dark blue reveal the original U.S. insignia underneath.

WWII Military Flight Goggles
A set of aviation goggles with heaven brown wool fleece on the edges. The goggles were worn during the war in the Aleutians.

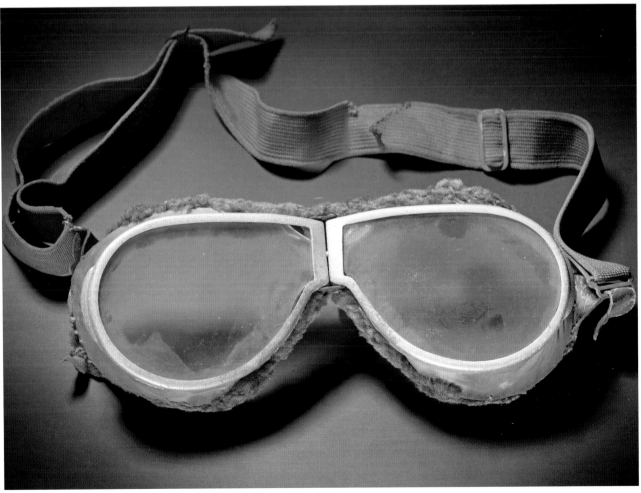

U.S. Army Air Forces Alaskan Suit
Alaska was an Arctic proving ground for extreme cold weather flying clothing and equipment. During World War II, the U.S. Army Air Forces issued to units operating in the region the "Alaskan Suit", consisting of a B-7 three-quarter-length jacket and A-6 trousers. The suit's shearling construction and wolf fur-trimmed hood combined with accessories such as the AN-H-16 heavy winter flying helmet kept the wearer comfortable in severe sub-zero temperatures.

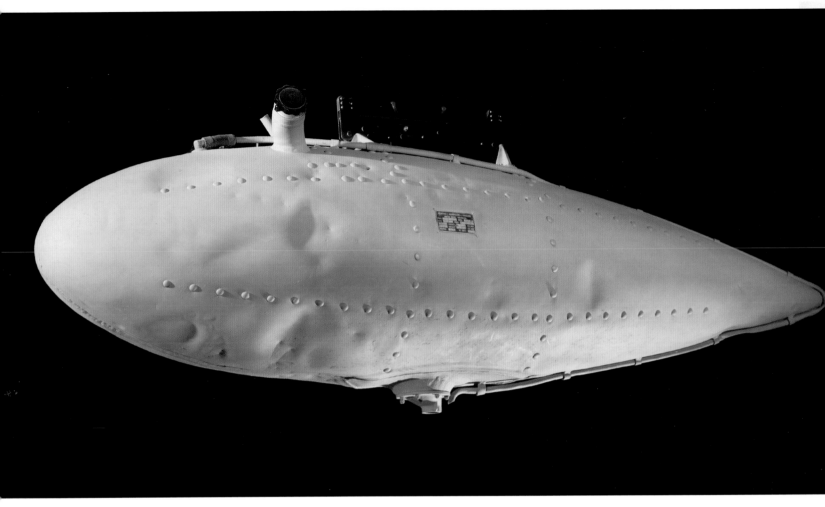

External Fuel Tank, P-40E Warhawk
U.S. Army Air Forces combat units used external fuel tanks to extend the operating range of fighters like the Curtiss P-40E Warhawk by hundreds of miles. Before entering combat, pilots jettisoned their "drop" tanks to increase maneuverability. The use of drop tanks was an absolute necessity in the Aleutians. They enabled long range missions between bases and targets. In the more numerous instances of bad weather and aborted missions, drop tanks gave an extra measure of safety as pilots often had to wait for breaks in heavy fog and rain to land.

Electric Flight Jacket
Military aircraft were unheated during World War II. Warm clothing that was flexible enough to allow crewmen to perform their duties was required in the intense cold. Electrified clothing was one solution to this problem.

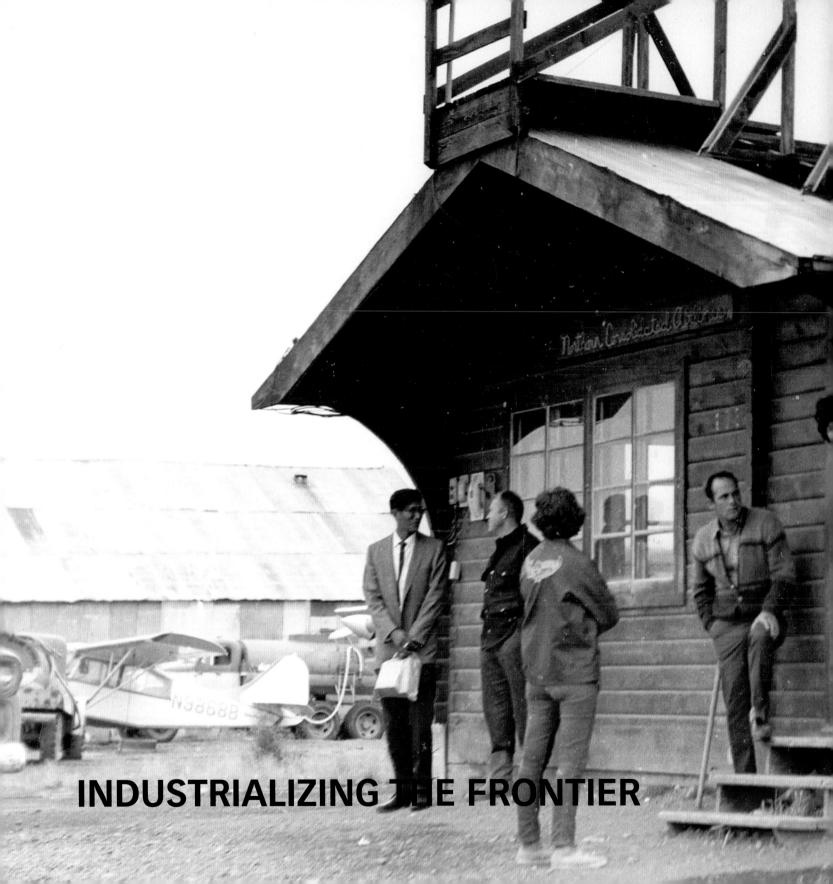

INDUSTRIALIZING THE FRONTIER

INDUSTRIALIZING THE FRONTIER

General Nathan Twining was Commander-in-Chief of the Alaskan Command in the late 1940s. In a statement before the Civil Aeronautics Board, he said Alaska was "itself a natural air theater [...]. As we picture it, the cities here are islands in the sea, just as divorced from each other as if out in the ocean."[55] To ensure the islands were properly linked, the Civil Aeronautics Administration (CAA) installed modern airports, overnight facilities for pilots and travelers, control towers, and hangars. Weather information was gathered from 150 different locations and broadcast to fliers from 49 stations. There was a major airport approximately every 150 miles, one airport for every 1,700 people in the Territory.[56]

When World War II ended, citizens of the Territory found that Alaska, with its imposed dependence upon aviation in all facets of life, had exactly what it most needed. The CAA spread word of the facilities available and encouraged both commercial and private pilots to try them. They recommended that all pilots headed to the North carry maps, guns, emergency rations, first-aid kits, matches, flares, and pocket compasses. Despite its modern airfields, Alaska was a dangerous place to fly and conditions required extensive survival knowledge.

Bob Reeve took advantage of the war surplus and bought military DC-3 airplanes for his new Reeve Airways. The men he hired were principally former Army fighter pilots fresh from combat. The business ventures of bush pilots were growing bigger. Ben Eielson spent his young life in pursuit of a dream that called for a network of airlines connecting Alaska to Asia and Europe. Noel Wien and his brothers later founded the prestigious Wien Airlines while Harold Gillam, using his uncanny ability to cope with the Territory's fickle weather, opened the way for development of early navigational

aids. Of course, despite those improvements, many bush pilots did not lose entirely their anti-establishment attitude. "I hate to fly off a tower-controlled airport," remarked Sam White. "I like to make my own decisions. The lakes and rivers make a better airport for me, for then I am on my own."[57]

The industrialization of Alaska and its aviation system was related not just to war but also to such factors as commercialization, government, resource development, and the environment. Alaska was always strategic for its minerals as well as its location. As everything became bigger – runways, airplanes, business, population – the stakes were bigger also. Resources became more precious. And, once again, the bush pilots took advantage of the opportunities with new advances in aeronautical technology.

Helicopters joined fixed-wing aircraft in Alaska after World War II. In 1948, pilot Carl Brady received a contract to fly mapping missions over Southeast, creating the first commercial helicopter operation. Brady mapped the southern portion of Chichagof Island in thirty-three days, whereas it had previously taken seven years to map the southern portion. Government agencies began increasingly to use helicopters. In 1956, Brady opened year-round helicopter operations at Anchorage's Merrill Field. In addition to transporting mapping and surveying crews, helicopters were also used for heavy-lift operations and medical evacuations.

The discovery of North Slope oil at Prudhoe Bay in 1969 had the oil companies flocking to Alaska. Anchorage became their Alaskan headquarters, hosting thirty-three companies. This surge in economic growth was most evident during the North Slope lease sales, when

This Certifies that
Robert Sanford
has crossed the

ARCTIC CIRCLE

as a passenger of the

Wien ALASKA *Airlines*

SINCE 1924

on the 12th day of August 1945
at 3 o'clock P.M.

WITNESSES: *Richard B. Webb*

LANDED AT *Shungnak*

Frank H. Whaley PILOT

As part of its service, Wien Alaska Airlines issued a special certificate to passengers that traveled across the Arctic Circle. Long-time Wien bush pilot Frank Whaley flew Robert Sanford of the U.S. Bureau of Mines to Shungnak, 150 miles east of Kotzebue in August 1945. Flights to rural areas like Shungnak meant take-offs and landings were from gravel strips and bars in rivers.

Bush pilot Jimmy Hoffman takes time out of his mail stops for Northern Consolidated Airlines to hand out bubble gum to children in the Alaska Native village of Eek, on the Kuskokwim River. Photo by Ward Wells.

Anchorage International Airport ramps and parking areas were full of corporate jets and when, due to the lack of accommodations, executives were forced to stay overnight in their aircraft. Once the lease sale was completed, the next project involved getting the oil to market. In 1974 Congress approved construction of the 800-mile-long Trans-Alaska Pipeline from Prudhoe Bay to Valdez, which spanned some of the most rugged terrain in the state. The Alyeska Pipeline Service Company, a cooperative venture of several oil corporations, completed the construction, and the oil began flowing in June of 1977. Again, Anchorage was the project's headquarters, and all traffic and supplies came through Anchorage via aircraft or ship.

To support the construction, aircraft carrying supplies flew in and out of fourteen new airstrips. Helicopters transported surveyors, engineers, inspectors, and others to remote sites. Interior Airways was the main operator on the North Slope before construction on the pipeline began. At the height of the oil boom they were employing hundreds of people to support their operations, flying Hercules, Otters, Boxcars, Norseman, Beavers, and other aircraft of military origin. ERA Aviation was the primary operator of twenty helicopters serving the North Slope.

Neither trapping nor mining was very profitable in the post-war years, yet change was coming. Signs of this change were making their way into remote corners of Alaska's interior. Helicopters were a noisy prelude to intense exploration for oil and other minerals. Plastic-wrapped loaves of bread were delivered by airplane to villages where grocery counters were still piled with furs. History was repeating itself. Mining companies wanted airplanes with skilled pilots to supply their operations. The airplane thus claimed victory over Alaska's ground transportation. Again bush pilots went to work, serving the needs of both villages and outsiders.

Airlines were now familiar to Alaskan travelers, and some that have now disappeared operated during the 1950s and 1960s. Pacific Northern Airways operated between Seattle and Anchorage, while Alaska Airlines was certified to operate from Seattle through Anchorage to Fairbanks. Cordova Airlines, which had served South Central Alaska, and Alaska Coastal Ellis Airlines, which had served Southeast Alaska with floatplanes, both merged with Alaska Airlines in the late 1960s.

Jets soon were introduced for commercial service. The improved technology caused a significant change in Alaskan air travel. Jets could fly over bad weather instead of around it and modern jets also decreased travel time. While a four-engine piston aircraft took six to eight hours to fly from Seattle to Anchorage, jets made the trip in three hours.

Northwest Orient Airlines introduced jet service on its flights through Alaska in 1960. In 1961, Alaska Airlines began the first commercial jetliner service between Alaska cities. Pan American Airways and Pacific Northern Airways soon followed.

The new aircraft required better landing facilities. The Federal Aid Airport Act of 1958 provided annual subsidies and the new State of Alaska in 1960 issued bonds for airport construction. In 1962, the legislature authorized the "bush program," which allowed for airport construction in remote communities. The "trunk program" provided construction funds for larger fields, though still in smaller villages. One included the Savoonga airport, which allowed the last dog-team mail route to be retired. In the early 1970s state-funded construction of airfields in Southeast Alaska made it possible for wheeled airplanes, at first small twin-engine aircraft and later jets, to replace a majority of the floatplanes that had been a mainstay.

As the 1980s began, most people traveling to and from Alaska did so in airplanes. Within the state, there were nearly as many airplanes registered to private owners as there were automobiles. By 1983, Alaska had seventy-two times as many commuter aircraft as the average of the rest of the states. The majority of passenger traffic in Alaska and much of the mail and freight traffic was airborne. Air commerce carried the equivalent of fifteen times the state's population each year. Alaska also became a possible space-shuttle location when Eielson Air Force Base outside Fairbanks was being considered as a possible emergency landing site for polar-orbiting shuttle flights.[58]

Not everyone, however, favored such development. Bush pilots bristled at government intervention and the tourist influx into the wilderness. Many wanted Alaska to remain a frontier and maintain

the territorial sensibility that fueled resistance to regulation. That spirit can be traced back to the early days when Bob Reeve and others came to Alaska to get away from the burdens of civilization. Clearly this outlook clashed with the emergence of big government. Pilots worried about the loss of access, revenue, and independence with the changes. A portion of a letter written by Sam White to Richard Wien on January 16, 1956, captures the Alaskan bush pilot's maverick way of thinking:

You and I are kindred spirits. We like the wide-open spaces. I wouldn't swap places with the automatons on the Outside for all the coffee in Brazil. In my visits Outside I have been asked, "How can you spend your life in such a desolate country? To my notion there is no such thing as desolate country in Alaska. The forests are full of beauty, the tundra has its majestic beauty, the lakes, the rivers, and the mountains and valleys all have beauty bestowed on them by God. They are all peopled by wild animals that are self-sufficient in their own right.

When man comes along with his 'improvements' and makes trails, rustic bridges over trickles of water, benches for people to rest on, his chest expands and his head gets bigger and he fancies that he has made a great improvement on the original. Phooey say I. I like the way it was in the beginning.[59]

The bush pilot culture bristled at the idea of government regulation, which meant they had to pass physical and mental tests to acquire a pilot's license and abide by rules restricting their movements and choices made in the air and on the ground. They expressed their freedom through flying whether they had a formal license, an overloaded bush plane, or safe equipment. Government officials first granted licenses to bush pilots wherever they found them, including riverbanks, lakes, and remote strips in the interior. The process was not without its problems. The pioneer fliers in Alaska influenced a cultural characteristic that is called "bush pilot syndrome" today.[60] Their heroic seat-of-the-pants flying encouraged many in later generations to adopt attitudes, habits, and procedures that emulated their get-the-job-done culture. In the process, they rejected the interference of government regulation and advances in technology while embracing a reasoning that justified bending and breaking the rules due to the special circumstances found in Alaska. All they needed was a bush plane and their ability to use their eyesight, intuition, and skill and they could get through any bad weather or rough terrain. These pilots believed that flying by what is called visual flight rules (VFR) today prevailed in all conditions. The use of any technology beyond the standard airplane was a nuisance.

Despite that heroic and individualist image, many bush pilots found plenty of opportunity within the increasingly formalized world of aviation and embraced technologies that made flying safer. Jorgy Jorgensen became a successful and famous pilot because he flew in both worlds. He used his Native experience to survive in all types of weather and terrain using VFR. At the same time, he excelled at flying "blind," called instrument flight rules (IFR), using new navigational

Wien flight attendants disembark from a Boeing 737.

technology introduced into the region after World War II. Reflecting his Native culture, Jorgensen believed that Mother Nature required the most knowledge, understanding, and respect regardless of whether he was flying by sight or by instruments. Flying by IFR simply increased survivability, which made it a valuable tool when needed, but it was not the only tool. Jorgensen advised:

If you're going to go out on the ice looking for something it's best to go on a clear night because you can see the stars and get something to navigate off, if you know your stars at all. So the pitch black is the best time to fly up in that country when you are expecting bad weather. Pick a good clear night when it is cold and the moon is out. The compass did not work that far north.[61]

The CAA and the organizational iterations that followed increasingly formalized and established a vital infrastructure that made modern aviation possible in Alaska. Besides regulation in the form of licensing, management of airways, and the authorization of commercial routes that fostered aerial entrepreneurship, the federal government worked to make navigating the air of Alaska safer. There was a continued tension between bush pilots, in many ways echoing criticisms voiced in the larger American general aviation community based on individual freedoms in the air, and the government in the form of the Federal Aviation Administration (FAA) after 1958. In response to the Civil Aeronautics Act, which assigned specific routes to specific pilots based on "grandfather rights," Reeve wrote:

If we pilots who made Alaska what it is today had waited until the outlying bush and mountain "required" airplane transportation by virtue of public convenience and necessity, this Territory would be today just about nothing but a worthless wilderness. The old-time Alaskan operator who made the country what it is was a man who made business where there had never been business before; he was a man who in most instances was forced to hustle and rustle or starve. It was the rustler who survived. I have deliberately gone prospecting with my airplane and discovered, staked and sold gold mining property at far below its actual value for the sole purpose of building up airplane transportation business to that district. On one property alone over $90,000 has been spent for transportation, wages, machinery, etc. Gentlemen, suppose I had waited until that district or any of those other districts required service by virtue of public convenience and necessity? IT would still be a wilderness [...]"[62]

Despite that tension, the special circumstances in Alaska related weather and terrain, led the FAA to partner with the University of Alaska at Anchorage and UPS Aviation Technologies to pioneer a new safety program called Capstone beginning in 1999. The leading cause of aircraft accidents are instances of pilots flying into bad weather and zero-visibility conditions only relying upon VFR – eyesight, intuition, and skill for navigation. Capstone paid for the installation of an avionics system that included a global positioning system (GPS) receiver and a multifunction display that reported aircraft position, course, speed, altitude, projected flight path, and weather, as well as the positions of other aircraft, to the pilot. On the ground, transceivers collected the data from each aircraft and broadcast the information to all similarly-equipped aircraft in the air and to a central FAA air traffic control center. The use of this network system, called Automatic Dependent Surveillance-Broadcast (ADS-B), cut accidents in half. The FAA expanded the program beyond Alaska and

A Federal Aviation Administration flight service station at the airport in Kotzebue, Alaska.

has stipulated that it be a core component of future aircraft in its new satellite-based Next Generation Air Transportation System (NextGen) system. Capstone also led directly to the rapid adoption of ADS-B as a principal means of air traffic control in other parts of the world, including Canada, Western Europe, China, and Australia.

As the Capstone program was taking shape, a tragic reminder of the need for such technology occurred. Former Alaska Senator Ted Stevens and three other passengers died in the crash of a bush plane on a mountainside near Aleknagik in southwest Alaska on August 9, 2010. The results of the official investigation were inconclusive, but it noted that the highly experienced pilot, Theron "Terry" Smith, who also died in the crash, had turned off the terrain awareness warning system that might have assisted with navigation through the mountains. Due to the varied Alaskan terrain, experienced bush pilots learned the system consistently alerted changes in elevation that were a natural part of the varied Alaskan landscape. Rather than flying with constant alerts, many turned the systems off, preferring to rely upon instinct.

While bush pilots and the federal government created networks in the air, others sought to present the Territory to outsiders. Alaska's pioneer appeal was an easy sell for marketers. Alaska's pilots and its landscape were something to export, similar to Romantic painters' depictions of remote wilderness a century earlier.

The 1950s, CBS television series *High Adventure with Lowell Thomas*, starring the famous journalist and explorer, dedicated an entire episode to the challenges and possibilities of Alaska as "America's last frontier" in October 1958. Thomas, joined by his son, Lowell

Thomas, Jr., used the airplane to show viewers the vast wilderness of the soon-to-be state in color. One of the segments featured Thomas landing on a glacier with "one of the best-known of the Alaskan daredevils," Noel Wien's son Merrill. Viewers clearly saw that in the absence of highways and railroads, the airplane became an integral part of the adventure of living in Alaska.[63]

Outsiders wanted a glimpse of wilderness, and bush pilots were able to make a living bringing them to a region they could experience it from the passenger seat of an airplane, their newly purchased gear and cameras shuttled by experienced pilots who provided them with a temporary adventure. Bush pilots also brought sightseers, hunters, and climbers to the ultimate symbol of the inaccessible North – the face of Mount McKinley. McKinley spawned such aviation specialties as mountain rescues, high-altitude flying, and glacier landings. Having become captivated by Alaska, Lowell Thomas, Jr., and his family stayed in Alaska. He flew his Helio Courier up and down the mountain for many years, which included a significant tenure as the owner of Talkeetna Air Taxi.

Early bush pilots came to Alaska in search of the wilderness that provides independence, an environment in which man was an interloper. The idea of the wilderness as place where the land is larger than the footprint of man does not exist as readily for the contemporary bush pilot. Today, Alaska offers some people an approximation of the wilderness and, for even fewer, something closer to the real thing – all by airplane. The same technology that allows one to "get away from it all" also provides easy access and, since the 1960s, has been instrumental in Alaska's losing much of its frontier innocence.

Flight Attendant Uniform, Wien Alaska Airlines
Noel Wien entered the airline business in 1927 in Nome, which made his the first in Alaska and one of the earliest in the United States. By the 1960s, Wien Air Alaska was an international air carrier that pioneered jet service to gravel runways and the use of "combi" aircraft capable of carrying both cargo and passengers. Flight attendant Diana Tuby wore this uniform during the last days of the airline before it closed down in 1985.

Alaska Flight Bags
The airline business was always a competitive one in Alaska. Featured here are vinyl flight bags produced by Alaska Airlines, Eliis Airlines, Pacific Northern Airlines, and Reeve Aleutian Airways, Inc.

16mm Bell and Howell Movie Camera
Movie camera, owned by Lowell Thomas, Jr. and used to film his travels to and around Alaska by airplane to show the rest of the country the "Last Frontier" as part of the popular television series of the 1950s entitled High Adventure.

Airline Advertisements
The air industry in Alaska was competitive since its earliest days. Early bush pilots competed for air routes, business and passengers. Advertisements like the ones shown here marketed air services to people within Alaska but also worked to sell Alaska as a destination by air to people outside the state.

Flying Boxcar

The Fairchild C-119 Flying Boxcar (Navy and Marine
Corps designation R4Q) was an American military
transport aircraft developed from the World War
II-era Fairchild C-82 Packet, designed to carry cargo,
personnel, litter patients, and mechanized equipment, and to drop cargo and troops by parachute.
The first C-119 made its initial flight in November
1947, and by the time production ceased in 1955,
more than 1,100 C-119s had been built. Its cargo-
hauling ability and unusual appearance earned it
the nickname "Flying Boxcar". Many C-119s flew
in Alaska for Northern Pacific Transport, Gifford
Aviation, Stebbins & Ambler Air Transport, and Delta
Associates. They were also used for public service
contracts, such as hauling building materials to the
villages in the bush of Alaska that have no road
access.

Nose Panel from Douglas DC-3 King Chris

In the early 1940s, the Civil Aeronautics Administration (CAA – the modern day Federal Aviation Administration) moved quickly to establish landing areas and radio ranges throughout Alaska for national defense. Pilot Jack T. Jeffords led the effort. In 1942, the CAA team received a twin-engine Douglas DC-3 airliner. They named it King Chris after their colleague, engineer Chris Lample, who was responsible for the design and construction of all of the CAA's landing and navigational facilities. Jeffords flew King Chris, the first DC-3 to fly in Alaska, to areas that were difficult for smaller and more maneuverable bush planes to fly.

Reeve Aleutian Airways Sign

*Well-known bush pilot Robert Reeve established
Reeve Aleutian Airways (RAA) in March 1947 with
a small fleet of surplus military transports he
converted into airliners. RAA provided service from
Anchorage to Attu at the westernmost tip of the
Aleutian Islands. Reeve's aircraft carried passengers, mail, and cargo, and proved instrumental
in connecting the people of the Aleutians to the
outside world. This sign hung at the Cold Bay
airport on the Alaskan Peninsula, which served as
an important hub for the airline until RAA ceased
operations in 2000.*

Capstone Cockpit Display Simulator

*Alaskan bush pilots face the challenge of unpredict-
able weather and rugged terrain every day. The
leading cause of aircraft accidents were instances
of pilots flying into bad weather and zero-visibility
conditions only relying upon their eyesight for
navigation. In 1999, the FAA initiated the Capstone
program, which paid for the installation of a GPS
system that broadcast aircraft position to ground-
based transceivers. They, in turn, transmitted back
the location of nearby aircraft and weather data.
The use of Automatic Dependent Surveillance-
Broadcast (ADS-B) technology in Alaska reduced
accidents by nearly half. This is a cockpit display
simulator from an early phase of Capstone.*

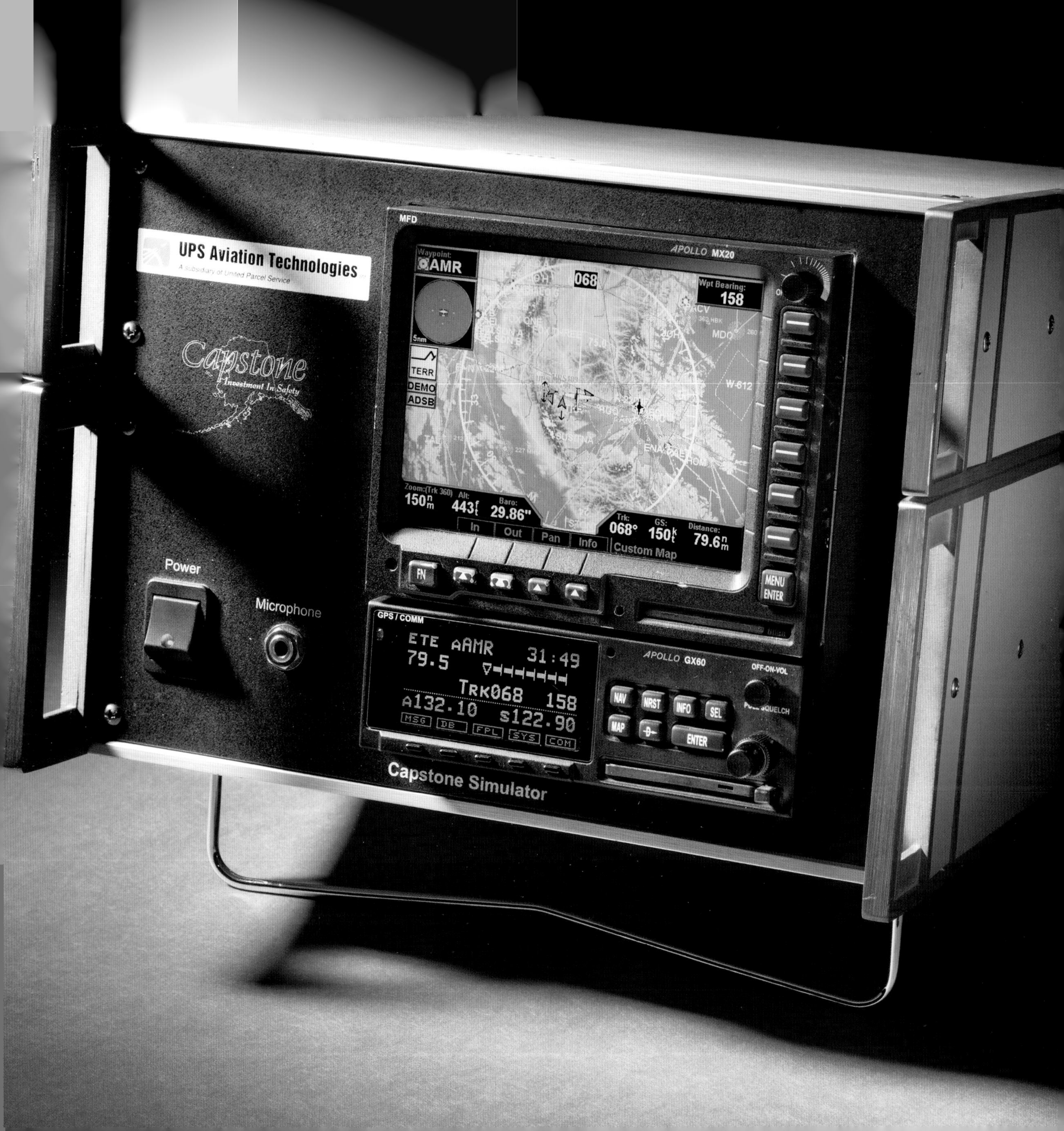
UPS Aviation Technologies
A subsidiary of United Parcel Service
Capstone
Investment In Safety
Power
Microphone
MFD
APOLLO MX20
GPS / COMM
APOLLO GX60
Capstone Simulator

CONCLUSION
A SECOND CENTURY IN THE AIR

The difference between the way I fly and the way the early bush pilots flew is that I have GPS, a cell phone, and weather reporting.

Paul Claus, bush pilot

As Alaska enters its second century of flight, three interrelated and dynamic constants remain. First, Alaska needs the airplane to survive. The arrival of the airplane in the 1920s circumvented and stalled the development of other transportation networks. As the airplane became an indispensable part of modern life around the world, it became central to Alaska. Second, there will always be a need for bush pilots to serve as a vital conduit between Alaska and the outside world. Finally, this frontier aerial state offers some of the most inhospitable weather and challenging terrain on the planet. Nature has not been conquered with improved technology, but pilots have been able to mitigate some of its harshest elements. In other words, nothing much has changed.

Alaska still serves as an important byway. Commercial flights continue to draw Europe and North America closer by carrying passengers and cargo. Even the American president's personal aerial transportation, *Air Force One*, uses the same routes to traverse the world as an instrument of diplomacy. That type of access brings many of the trappings of the modern world to the state making it a bit more like the rest of the world.

After one hundred years of aviation in Alaska, the conditions discovered by Eielson, Wien, Reeve, Jorgenson, and others remain. Alaska is a place of wild extremes with wind and snow, rugged terrain, and far-flung villages unconnected by roads – a place where the best practical means for travel and freight is the airplane. Air travel, now, as in the past, is critical to everyday life.

Anchorage, the state's largest city and home to half of Alaska's total population, still has only one major road leading north and another leading south. You cannot drive to Nome or Juneau. Aviation has created a dependence of Alaskans on the sky. At the end of the twenty-first century, Alaska is likely to still be an inaccessible state of isolated cities and villages. Change, however, may not be the best gauge. For it is not in the air that the airplane has made a difference; it is on the ground, where people in rural Alaska still greet the airplane, anxiously awaiting their mail, fresh food, and a glimpse of the pilot. Today, Alaskans fly thirty times more per capita than other U.S. citizens. The growth of Alaskan aviation is without parallel, but flying in Alaska is far from being a spectacle. It is the necessity of the North.

WORKS CITED

Amundsen, Roald, and Lincoln Ellsworth. First Crossing of the Polar Sea. Garden City, N.Y.: Doubleday, 1928.

"Army Fliers Home From Alaska Trip." New York Times, October 21, 1920. pg. 10.

Bertorelli, Paul. "Ted Stevens Crash: A Nasty Reminder." August 16, 2010. www.avweb.com/blogs/insider/AVWebInsider_StevensCrash_203140-1.html (Accessed August 2, 2012).

Calkins, Annie. Alaska's Heritage, Chapters 4-12: Air Transportation. 2012. Alaska Humanities Forum. Alaska History and Culture Studies. www.akhistorycourse.org/articles/article.php?artID=177 (Accessed July 9, 2012).

Corn, Joseph J. The Winged Gospel: America's Romance with Aviation. London: Oxford University Press, 1983. Reprint, Baltimore: Johns Hopkins, 2001.

Courtwright, David. T. Sky as Frontier: Adventure, Aviation, and Empire. College Station: Texas A&M University Press, 2005.

"Danger in the Arctic: Joe Crosson, Aviator." True Comics 4 (1941): 12–21.

Day, Beth. Glacier Pilot: The Story of Bob Reeve and the Flyers Who Pushed Back Alaska's Air Frontiers. New York: Holt, 1957.

Driscoll, Joseph. War Discovers Alaska. New York: J.B. Lippincott, 1943.

Garfield, Brian. The Thousand-Mile War: World War II in Alaska and the Aleutians. New York: Doubleday, 1969. Reprint, Fairbanks: University of Alaska Press, 1995.

Glines, Carroll V. Around the World in 175 Days: The First Round-the-World Flight. Washington, D.C.: Smithsonian Institution Press, 2001.

Greiner, James. Wager with the Wind: The Don Sheldon Story. New York: St. Martin's, 1974.

Gwynn-Jones, Terry. Farther and Faster: Aviation's Adventuring Years, 1909–1939. Washington, D.C.: Smithsonian Institution Press, 1991.

Harkey, Ira. Noel Wien: Alaska Pioneer Bush Pilot. Fairbanks: U of Alaska P, 1974.

Haugen, W.A. "Lowell Thomas High Adventure Photos." March 2008. http://webpost.atwebpages.com/Thomas/photos.htm (Accessed July 1, 2012).

Heaslip, William T. "Retractable Aircraft Landing Element Mounting." U.S. Patent No. 2,925,970. February 23, 1960.

Hummel, Laurel J. "The U.S. Military as Geographical Agent: The Case of Cold War Alaska." The Geographical Review 95 (January 2005): 47–72.

Janson, Lone E. Mudhole Smith: Alaska Flier. Anchorage, AK: Alaska Northwest, 1981.

Jorgenson, Holger, and Jean Lester. Jorgy: The Life of Native Alaskan Bush Pilot and Airline Captain Holger "Jorgy" Jorgensen. Ester, AK: Ester Republic, 2008.

Leonard, Frank M. "High Adventure with Lowell Thomas: Alaska High Fliers." October 8, 1958. http://webpost.atwebpages.com/Thomas/PDFs/LTHAAlaskaMerrillWien10-8-1958.pdf (Accessed July 3, 2012).

Leonard, Frank M. "High Adventure with Lowell Thomas: Piqued by Peak." October 8, 1958. http://webpost.atwebpages.com/Thomas/PDFs/LTHAAlaska-Mountains10-8-1958.pdf (Accessed July 3, 2012).

Maurer, Maurer. Aviation in the U.S. Army, 1919–1939. Washington, D.C.: Office of Air Force History, 1987.

Mohler, Stanley R., and Bobby H. Johnson. Wiley Post, His Winnie Mae, and the World's First Pressure Suit. Washington, D.C.: Smithsonian Institution Press, 1971.

"Nome Flyers Plan Crossing to Siberia." New York Times, August 26, 1920. pg. 13.

"Norge Badly Damaged." The Washington Post, May 19, 1926. pg. 3.

Owen, Russell. "Called the Greatest Feat of Aviation," New York Times, April 22, 1928, pg. 1.

Page, Dorothy G. Polar Pilot: The Carl Ben Eielson Story. Danville, Ill.: Interstate Publishers, 1992.

Post, Wiley, and Harold Gatty. Around the World in Eight Days: The Flight of the Winnie Mae. New York: Rand-McNally, 1931).

Rearden, Jim. Sam O. White, Alaskan: Tales of a Legendary Wildlife Agent and Bush Pilot. Missoula, MT: Pictorial Histories, 2007.

Richfield, Paul. "Tundra Tire Nation." Flying (September 13, 2005). www.flyingmag.com/tundra-tire-nation (Accessed August 7, 2012).

Ringsmuth, Katie. "Wranegll Mountain Skyboys: Making History Above Alaska's Copper Belt." Publication manuscript, 2012.

Rogers, Will. "Will Rogers Sees Alaska As a Democratic Heaven." New York Times, August 9, 1935, pg. 19.

Sherwood, Morgan. "The End of Wilderness." Environmental Review 9 (Fall 1985): 197–209.

Smith, Blake W. Warplanes to Alaska. Surrey, B.C.: Hancock House, 1998.

Smith, Blake W. Wings Over the Wilderness: They Flew the Trail of '42. Surrey, B.C.: Hancock House, 2008.

Stevens, Robert W. Alaskan Aviation History. Vol. 1-2. Des Moines, Wash.: Polynyas Press, 1990.

Streett, St. Clair. "The First Alaskan Air Expedition." National Geographic Magazine 41 (May 1922): 445-552.

Tordoff, Dirk. Mercy Pilot: The Joe Crosson Story. Portland, OR: Epicenter, 2002.

Volz, Matt. "Alaska Officials Target Bush Pilots' Culture to Reduce Crashes." Associated Press. September 7, 2004. http://archives.californiaaviation.org/pilot/msg00093.html (Accessed August 1, 2012).

Wilkins, George H. Flying the Arctic. New York: G.P. Putnam's Sons, 1928.

Wilkins, George H. "Wilkins Flies From Alaska to Spitsbergen in 20 ½ Hours." New York Times, April 22, 1928, pg. 1.

NOTES

[1] There have been reports of an earlier flight with a homegrown airplane in Nome in 1912, but they have not been confirmed.

[2] Corn, 12.

[3] Courtwright, 6.

[4] Ringsmuth, 6-13.

[5] Maurer, 176.

[6] Army aviation went through several organizational names since its beginning in 1907. It was known as the Air Service (1918-1926), Air Corps (1926–1942), and Air Forces (1942–1947), before officially becoming the U.S. Air Force in 1947.

[7] Streett, 552; Maurer, 174-176; "Nome Flyers Plan Crossing to Siberia," 13.

[8] "Army Fliers Home from Alaska Trip," 10.

[9] Maurer, 352-354.

[10] Amundsen and Ellsworth, First Crossing of the Polar Sea; "Norge Badly Damaged," 3.

[11] Wilkins, Flying the Arctic; Owen, "Called the Greatest Feat of Aviation," 1; Wilkins, "Wilkins Flies From Alaska to Spitsbergen in 20 1/2 Hours," 1.

[12] Rogers, "Will Rogers See Alaska as a Democratic Heaven," 19.

[13] Day, 20.

[14] Harkey, 68.

[15] Day, 20.

[16] Rearden, 135.

[17] Day, 20.

[18] Rearden, 128.

[19] Day, 193.

[20] Day, 20.

[21] Harkey, 133.

[22] Harkey, 133.

[23] Tordoff, 202.

[24] Tordoff, 203.

[25] Jorgensen and Lester, 19–20.

[26] Rearden, 237.

[27] Jorgensen and Lester, 54.

[28] Jorgensen and Lester, 15.

[29] Jorgensen and Lester, 54.

[30] Jorgensen and Lester, 56.

[31] Day, 21.

[32] Day, 169.

[33] Day, 112.

[34] Day, 112.

[35] Tordoff, 161.

[36] Greiner, 79.

[37] Greiner, 83.

[38] Greiner, 93.

[39] Day, 178.

[40] Calkins.

[41] Jorgensen and Lester, 16.

[42] Day, 76.

[43] Harkey, 102.

[44] Day, 75.

[45] Day, 178.

[46] Day 178.

[47] Rearden, 245.

[48] Richfield, "Tundra Tire Nation."

[49] Richfield.

[50] Garfield, 349.

[51] Tordoff, 229.

[52] Rearden, 255.

[53] Day, 284.

[54] Hummel, 50.

[55] Day, 285.

[56] Day, 285.

[57] Rearden, 274.

[58] Calkins.

[59] Rearden, 357.

[60] Volz, "Alaska Officials Target Bush Pilots' Culture to Reduce Crashes"; Bertorelli, "Ted Stevens Crash: A Nasty Reminder."

[61] Jorgensen and Lester, 10.

[62] Day, 186.

[63] Leonard, "High Adventure with Lowell Thomas: Alaska High Fliers," and "High Adventure with Lowell Thomas: Piqued by Peak," October 8, 1958; Haugen, "Lowell Thomas High Adventure Photos."

CREDITS